EXPLORING
CONFIDENCE!!!

JOHN KENNEDY

authorHOUSE®

AuthorHouse™ UK
1663 Liberty Drive
Bloomington, IN 47403 USA
www.authorhouse.co.uk
Phone: 0800.197.4150

Published by AuthorHouse 03/02/2018

ISBN: 978-1-5462-8934-0 (sc)
ISBN: 978-1-5462-8935-7 (hc)
ISBN: 978-1-5462-8936-4 (e)

CONTENTS

This book is dedicated to my mother Kate.
I can never thank you enough for the love and
encouragement you have given me
Throughout my life

PROLOGUE

Unbelievably so many views in life really can surround us all so let us become involved around the importance at this beginning when undergoing every dramatic spring day of the start we are discussing, when I emerged from this room at Kings College Hospital of London so knowing at provision which once reaching 6.00a.m conformably that would next be for looking up at regular involvement from having undergone more surgery experienced providing hopeful emotions giving personal health new life for a successful future to become number seventeen along we go plus in we visit over for electrical wires and machinery to be inserted in and throughout everything which shall come up and be discussed with you bringing in sudden disbelief but great success to certain unbelievable stories.

Well after excepting surgery everything arrived to be awake throughout with confidence rolled out making sure body stiffened up bringing psychological strength into the mind enabling the first tests to begin and suddenly reach out shaking just like a CAT Scan shall explain later of which caused me to have some seizures eventually that ended and went on.

Eventually the giggling sensation would now have to be constantly explained and studied at hospitals. Somehow this was a kind of tingly stomach sensation. Unfortunately there seemed to be no understanding. As to what was causing these tickly and tingling sensations. Next in this story, I go on to writing about how I would constantly be describing the giggling. "They are like a kind of tingling in the centre nerve of my stomach. "If you count to ten it is as if they are like the speed of your heartbeat." I would be saying.

So these evil things would start dramatically one, two, three, four, five, six, seven, eight, nine and ten. Suddenly the tingling sensation went a lot stronger in the centre of my chest. Then my voice tone would suddenly rise to a much higher level. I explained they were like somebody going "Boo!!" and making you jump out of your skin. Another way to explain this strangely enough was "That it is like a person having butterflies in there stomach" my mum would actually also explain to hospitals. Well after the studying by Dr Patterson, plus me having visited Hallam hospital. I was next to move on and explain all of this again to many other hospitals.

Firstly, I was going on into the Children's hospital of Ladywood in Birmingham. But still not understanding I was to still be having to constantly repeat myself again and again with Doctors and neurologists. "Doctor, Doctor, I am getting this tingling sensation in my stomach. "It is like a heart beat where it tingles in my stomach. "Like a kind of sensation when you jump out of your skin." I would again say.

Often I would have these tickling feelings in my stomach at the hospital. While at other times the giggling would be at school or somewhere else in Birmingham. When these ticking and tingling sensations started in the centre of my stomach. Somehow it would suddenly make my tone of voice increase. Sometimes "I felt so stupid constantly they were making me sound like a little girl!" I would often be saying to my mum and doctors.

Well by now my consultant was Dr J. Varley, neurologist at the Children's hospital. While my family and me were at the hospital; "We are concerned about Lee. "Because from about the age of nine months he has had laughing attacks, he says he can have as many as six a day. "They begin with his eyes opening wide and he appears afraid."

This Dr. J. Varley would also be saying while still writing his information down. "They last a few seconds and suddenly he laughs, not a happy laugh which goes on for around 10-20 seconds. "Occasionally he has a temper after these episodes. "Lee can abort the turns by clenching his fists and he seems to dislike them." Dr J. Varley also then mentioned;

"It is quite clear that Phenobarbitone reduced the number of episodes. But he has not had any for twelve months."

Also mentioned was "We have also noticed that occasionally after eating, lee has a red linear flush on the left side of his face. "The flush is about three quarters of an inch wide. It runs from the lower part of the ear to the left cheek bone by the side of his mouth. "Generally Lee is an active boy who enjoys outdoor play." My mum Kate then said. Well unexpectedly "My impression is that lee's laughing episodes are an epileptic phenomenon and I have seen a boy with similar behaviour due to epilepsy – you will remember that he did well on Carbamazepine and I hope lee will do the same. Dr. J. Varley then said. Next "However, before starting this I would be grateful if lee could have another EEG here." then Dr J. Varley finished.

Well, on our next visit in the late 1970's, "Lee's EEG is normal, never the less as you know. I have suggested that he have Carbamazepine 100mg." Dr. J. Varley said. So now more medication!! This by taking diazepam in the morning and also at night.

We left the hospital and went back home to the Scott Arms. Next day just getting on and enjoying my life, wondering what the hell am I doing taking these tablets.

They are doing nothing for me and I do not have a health problem. My family regularly told me never let your misfortunes take over your life and never cry about them of which I do not ever do.

Bobby Charlton

Bobby Robson & Me for book

Colin West with Bob Taylor with my on my 21st birthday

Cyril Regis and me in Macro 1979

Dad, Granddad Geoff and me at World Cup Finals of 1990 in Naaples of Italy

Grandad Karol

Great Grandparients Grice

Jeff Astle and Me

KEVIN kEGAN AND ME

Me at North Portico

CHAPTER ONE

STARTING LIFE

Asleep or Awake

First stop became in Times Square where we all underwent talks concerning surgery "Lee, we have to explain your epilepsy is very rare we need to see you have an epileptic seizure so just enabling us to know where the tumour is involving in your hippocampus then for all of us next after minutes and time one through wires and tests becoming charged with all."

Well after excepting surgery everything arrived to be awake throughout with confidence rolled out making sure body stiffened up bringing psychological strength into the mind enabling the first tests to begin and suddenly reach out shaking just like a CAT Scan shall explain later of which caused me to have some seizures eventually that ended and went on.

Next everything started by going along into another room and so while lying on a bed surgeons inserted a metal box around my skull. I had four pain killer injections inserted into my head and then I lay back in the operating theatre. The surgeons then had work to do whilst me well lying on the medical bed for success to bring some new and happy life.

Expectable I was hardly in denial "that I faced a real and shocking experience to my life because the first symptoms of what would prove to be a non-malignant brain tumour confirmed a few years earlier by Professor Polkey and Mr Richard Selway on computer to me in Kings plus futurising the Mayo Clinic in Phoenix Arizona around more.

Interesting for success and needs for the New York Downtown hospital to which became a very needed computer on the 9.11 bombing of the World Trade Centre in Manhattan of New York reached out still since the incident on the 01st well this medical building had been the closest hospital to hospital for the bombing of the two upper buildings dragged along.

Why is that people say when discussing you have Neurological, along or maybe Psychology adding involvement to many others such as mentioned epilepsy and many more the medical doctors really care what do you say or do so many people in families look and so are always concerned but General Public what is that some Joke time to learn come on we all really do there are so many advantages for people to see and learn sports are fantastic but so many situations along with this should really be discussed personal thoughts of the health service is great but the public please learn medical problems are something not to ignore.

Family support

Along whilst observed each day regular support always brings strength into the mind tests and involvement of the past with present also reach on converged around me thinking of all the help I have had from my Mum, plus Natalie, alongside my Aunty Diane and Thomas my brother.

Natalie and I have been able to enjoy early Constantly support especially exhilarating summers and winters. This after and around my thrilling and exciting visiting out to New York. Where I was to walk the streets of Times Square in Manhattan to enjoy New Year's Eve and bring in so much time.

So then back to Tuesday, April 24, 2007, and after about twenty minutes I was taken into another operating theatre where I was then to undergo major brain surgery. While in the room I knew something was going on because at that moment I could feel something in my skull but at the same time many injections. Suddenly I then experienced two or three epileptic seizures. One of which had been bad in the first operating theatre and somehow the other two being facial seizures in the second room. After around four hours I was then taken out of the theatre and into another ward where nurses were to keep an eye on me.

I also then tried to relax sleeping throughout the afternoon eventually starting to feel better. Had a read of my newspaper the USA Today plus West Bromwich Albion book and then eventually after taking my tablets I clocked out soon after eleven in the evening. Knowing through so much confidence how much along with medical help success would arrive that this operation had worked and cured me of this neuron disorder.

Next day, Wednesday 25th April 2007, I woke up in the Polkey ward at Kings another time being the New York Downtown hospital I then had my breakfast and at 6.00am after having had my blood pressure taken. Next on I went into another department in the hospital for a brain scan to see how my health was doing. After that I was then taken back to the Polkey ward where I stayed until mid-afternoon. Then I was taken into another channel where I hopefully was about to start my new life. Suddenly though while sleeping I felt as though my eyes twitched once, oh dear then time came for me to go back to sleep.

Next, on Thursday 26th April 2007, I was woken up again early to have my blood pressure taken regularly.

Throughout the day I just lay in bed reading the papers transferred from the States like the New York Times and the Dallas Morning News and San Francisco Chronicle whilst viewing the television later many political friends arrived with family for support Mum and Howard plus Tony Blair came to see me and we all had a good laugh. But at 5.45pm, I was reading the Readers Digest and Nursing Times but suddenly my eyes twitched twice. What was going on?

Then when waking on Friday 27th April 2007, it was my thirty-sixth birthday. But unfortunately I was still in Kings of London soon though to be the New York hospitals. On the afternoon my Mum and Howard came over and gave me some cards and new shirts. Later I just watched the television BBC news and read another the San Francisco Chronicle newspaper. Misfortune arrived because at 9.24pm, I had another very short facial epileptic seizure.

What is going on well on Saturday 28th April 2007, I extraordinarily with misfortune suddenly went into what I assumed was quite a long epileptic seizure. But so different as to what they were before the surgery because it felt like a slow muscle spasm seizure.

Then as usual the seizure again seemed to go on for quite a while lasting around twenty minutes. By now causing myself a lot of stress and thinking to myself. What the in high sky is going on! Well obviously what had happened was Mr Selway had done brain surgery on me. Then reducing the size of my brain tumour. So instead of me having strong fast Grand Mal Epileptic Seizures. What had happened was he had now done an operation on the left temporal lobe of my brain.

Now reducing the amount of my brain tumour which was causing the epilepsy. So I was now having a very short slow motion or speeded epileptic seizure.

Finally I left the hospital on Tuesday 1st May 2007, after having spent another three days at soon to be New York Down town now to come back home to Manhattan. Thinking well I have had the operation but assuming I was still having some kind of epileptic seizure so had anything worked?

One of the many things that my mother instilled in me is discipline. I have been taught never to give up, never to passively accept fate, but to exhaust every last ounce of will and hope in the face of any challenge. It has fuelled my determination as to whatever the subject. As to everybody in my family whatever and wherever frankly, it makes me furious. I am a realist, and have heard so much news throughout my life. I don't expect to be treated with a kids gloves. But I do believe in hope. And I believe that approaching adversity with a positive attitude at least gives you a chance of success. Approaching it with a defeatist attitude predestines the outcome: defeat. And a defeatist's attitude is just not of myself.

I respect the seriousness of epilepsy – I've had many situations as to where I have witnessed and seen some quite shocking moments but at the same time some amazing moments in life.

First stop became in Times Square where we all underwent talks concerning surgery "Lee, we have to explain your epilepsy is very rare we need to see you have an epileptic seizure so just enable us to know where the tumour is involving your brain so then for all of us next after minutes and time one through wires and tests became caused with all.

Well after excepting surgery everything arrived to be awake throughout with confidence rolled out making sure body stiffened up bringing psychological strength into the mind enabling the first tests to begin and suddenly reach out shaking just like a CAT Scan shall explain later of which caused me to have some seizures eventually that ended and went on.

Next everything started by going along into another room and so while lying on a bed surgeons inserted a metal box around my skull. I had four pain killer injections inserted into my head and then I lay back in the operating theatre. The surgeons then had work to do whilst me well lying on the medical bed for success to bring some new and happy life.

Expectable I was hardly in denial "that I faced a grave and shocking experience to my life because the first symptoms of what would prove to be a non-malignant brain tumour had been confirmed a few years earlier by Professor Polkey and Mr Richard Selway on computer to me in Kings plus futurizing the Mayo Clinic in Phoenix Arizona around more.

Interesting for success and needs for the New York Downtown hospital to which became a very needed computer on the 9.11 bombing of the World Trade Centre in Manhattan of New York reached out still since the incident on the 01st.

What are brain tumours you may ask?

Unbelievably then well it is something that can be looked or thought of as an epileptic seizure which damaged neurons cause epilepsy whilst a malignant brain tumour is classed as cancer. So two forms of brain tumours where a malignant tumour spreads and the non-malignant does not.

Well even though having that news life still seemed especially good at the same time. This was all confirmed while I was just about to start my relationship with Natalie bringing this interesting life along very medically rare whilst plenty of success inside and out through some very imported operation whilst fun and enjoyment arrives each day.

Regular support always brings strength into the mind the best hopes of the past and present also reach on converged around me. Thinking of all the help I have had from my Mum (Kate) plus Magda, alongside my Aunty Diane and Thomas my brother.

Success brings the ability to enjoy early socialisation back up especially exhilarating summers and winters. This after and around my thrilling and exciting visiting out to New York. Where I was to walk the streets of Times Square in Manhattan to enjoy New Year's Eve and bring in so much time.

So then back to Tuesday, April 24, 2007, and after about twenty minutes I was taken into another operating theatre where I was then to undergo major brain surgery. While in the room I knew something was going on because at that moment I could feel something in my skull but at the same time many injections. Suddenly I then experienced two or three epileptic seizures. One of which had been bad in the first operating theatre and somehow the other two being facial seizures in the second room. After around four hours I was then taken out of the theatre and into another ward where nurses were to keep an eye on me.

I also then tried to relax sleeping throughout the afternoon eventually starting to feel better. Had a read of my newspaper the USA Today plus West Bromwich Albion book and then eventually after taking my tablets I clocked out soon after eleven in the evening. Knowing through so much confidence how much along with medical help success would arrive that this operation had worked and cured me of epilepsy.

Next day, Wednesday 25th April 2007, I woke up in the Polkey ward at Kings another time being the New York Downtown hospital I then had my breakfast and at 6.00am after having had my blood pressure taken. Next on I went into another department in the hospital for a brain scan to see how my health was doing. After that I was then taken back to the Polkey ward where I stayed until mid-afternoon. Then I was taken into another channel where I hopefully was about to start my new life. Suddenly though while sleeping I felt as though my eyes twitched once, oh dear then time came for me to go back to sleep.

Next, on Thursday 26th April 2007, I was woken up again early to have my blood pressure taken regularly.

Throughout the day I just lay in bed reading the papers transferred from the States like the New York Times and the Dallas Morning News and San Francisco Chronicle whilst viewing the television later many political friends arrived with family for support Mum and Howard plus Tony Blair came to see me and we all had a good laugh. But at 5.45pm, I was reading the Readers Digest and Nursing Times but suddenly my eyes twitched twice. What was going on?

Then when waking on Friday 27th April 2007, it was my thirty-sixth birthday. But unfortunately I was still in Kings of London soon though to be the New York hospitals. On the afternoon my Mum and Howard came over and gave me some cards and new shirts. Later I just watched the television BBC news and read another the San Francisco Chronicle newspaper. Misfortune arrived because at 9.24pm, I had another very short facial epileptic seizure.

What is going on well on Saturday 28th April 2007, I extraordinarily with misfortune suddenly went into what I assumed was quite a long epileptic seizure. But so different as to what they were before the surgery because it felt like a slow muscle spasm seizure.

Then as usual the seizure again seemed to go on for quite a while lasting around twenty minutes. By now causing myself a lot of stress and thinking to myself. What the in high sky is going on! Well obviously what had happened was Mr Selway had done brain surgery on me. Then reducing the size of my brain tumour. So instead of me having strong fast Grand Mal Epileptic Seizures. What had happened was he had now done an operation on the left temporal lobe of my brain.

Now reducing the amount of my brain tumour which was causing the epilepsy. So I was now having a very short slow motion or speeded epileptic seizure.

Finally I left the hospital on Tuesday 1st May 2007, after having spent another three days at soon to be New York Down town now to come back home to Manhattan. Thinking well I have had the operation but assuming I was still having some kind of epileptic seizure so had anything worked?

One of the many things that my mother instilled in me is discipline. I have been taught never to give up, never to passively accept fate, but to exhaust every last ounce of will and hope in the face of any challenge. It has fuelled my determination as to whatever the subject. As to everybody in my family whatever and wherever frankly, it makes me furious. I am a realist, and have heard so much news throughout my life. I don't expect to be treated with a kids gloves. But I do believe in hope. And I believe that approaching adversity with a positive attitude at least gives you a chance of success. Approaching it with a defeatist attitude predestines the outcome: defeat. And a defeatist's attitude is just not of myself.

I respect the seriousness of epilepsy – I've had many situations as to where I have witnessed and seen some quite shocking moments but at the same time some amazing moments in life.

Well health Services and hospitals involving EEG tests or MRI plus CAT Scans I have experienced them all. Scans well I have seen them all. To start I was born in Pensvania Avenue Dudley Road hospital in Birmingham of the West Midlands in the United Kingdom.

But unexpectedly my health and life has belonged into recovery but strong like a solder family call me went back and forth from all stages of life. Whilst also at the same time many superb experiences were to come along the way hoped sometimes the health would become involved.

Birmingham is my true home, but it is not my present home. At the time of my birth on Saturday 27, 71, the family and I would go around England and Europe while we lived at our Maisonette in Great Barr. We lived there in spring for ten years after I was born.

My mothers name is Kate. I am her one and only son. I have many Aunties and one is very special. Her name is Diane she is my mum's twin sister our family is quite large. My Aunty Diane and I are both very close along with her son Thomas. I class him as my little or big brother as he is now becoming this great goalkeeper.

My mother saved many mementos of my birth, as she does of her life back in West Bromwich. Many of which I still have on photographs back at home.

Had a chat recently "We would go to and from Central or even Buckingham two of the very special parks the other side of the world from each other." mum said. "This was only one minute up the road from the family house. Suddenly, lee I then noticed something about you!" Mum next mentioned. "You started to have episodes where voice tone would rise then you would giggle. This would be while you were asleep or awake. Then you would become upset out in frustration. Eventually I took you to Hallem Hospital. In Birmingham Lee to see a paediatrician." "Oh right mum!" I said. Then we finished our conversation.

Well in 1974, mum and me went off to see a Dr Patterson. He was my General Practitioner in Great Barr. By now explained: "I saw this little baby in the Out Patient Department with his mother, he has a history of hysterical laughter attacks during which he becomes uptight, this episode is followed by crying. "He has had up to six attacks a day, his mother says that he never falls down or loses consciousness. "She would not give me any history of him staring or appearing blank although I see that she confirmed this to you. "The attacks usually occur when he is quiet. "His past history was normal and he has reached his milestones at the normal age. "There is no family history of epilepsy. "On his examination there were no abnormal signs. "Unfortunately, I did not see an attack while talking to his family in the room." Dr Patterson was saying. "He is certainly young for these attacks to be epileptic, yet this would seem to be the only explanation. "I have decided to try the effect of phenobarbital (phenobarbitone) and I have prescribed this in a dose of 15 mgs b.d. "He can come again in three weeks' time for a review." Dr Patterson then finished.

So three weeks later, mum and I went again to visit Dr Patterson. Still I visited Hallem Hospital, but now to be advised. That we should visit another doctor named Dr Jeeves at Hallam hospital.

Strangely hospitals and doctors did not witness an epileptic seizure, but started to state that they think it must be epilepsy. Well I was too young to remember this. While at the same time, not sure what was going on in the hospital.

Even though hoping the doctors would be able to help my family and me.

By now the year was 1975, and I would be living as a cheerful young lad. I look back and start to remember things at around the age of four. Like my Great Grandad Grice where I was sitting in his rocking chair in West Bromwich. Plus also the sounds of "Hello Lee!" of which my Grandad would say. This while beginning my life living with my group futurising our independent flat on the Hillside Road at the Scott's area of Barr in the northern part of Brum.

One of my very special memories was especially at the age of three to four. When playing with my best mate Parsley. A Jack Russell dog, he was my Aunty Diane's dog.

They both regularly stayed with us. Now then my one very special memory is at Hillside Road there Parsley and me were sitting together playing on the floor with toys.

Itching Neurons

Eventually the giggling sensation would now have to be constantly explained and studied at hospitals. Somehow this was a kind of tingly stomach sensation. Unfortunately there seemed to be no understanding. As to what was causing these tickly and tingling sensations.

Next in this story, I go on to writing about how I would constantly be describing the giggling. "They are like a kind of tingling in the centre nerve of my stomach. "If you count to ten it is as if they are like the speed of your heartbeat." I would be saying.

So these evil things would start dramatically one, two, three, four, five, six, seven, eight, nine and ten. Suddenly the tingling sensation went a lot stronger in the centre of my Chest and next my voice tone would suddenly rise to a much higher level. I explained they were like somebody having itchy neurons!!" and making you psychologically confused inside your body. Another way to explain this strangely enough was "That it is like a person having butterflies in there stomach" my mum would actually also explain to hospitals.

Well after the studying by Dr Patterson, plus me having visited Hallam hospital. I was next to move on and explain all of this again to many other hospitals.

Firstly, I was going on into the Children's hospital of Ladywood in Birmingham. But still not understanding I was to still be having to constantly repeat myself repeatedly and again with Doctors and neurologists. "Doctor, Doctor, I am getting this itchy nerve sensation in my stomach. "It is like a heartbeat where it tingles in my stomach. "Like a kind of sensation when you jump out of your skin." I would again say.

Often I would have these tickling feelings in my stomach at the hospital. While at other times the giggling would be at school or somewhere else in Birmingham. When these ticking and tingling sensations started in the centre of my stomach. Somehow it would suddenly make my tone of voice increase. Sometimes "I felt so stupid constantly they were making me sound like a little girl! With a high toned voice" I would often be saying to my mum and doctors.

Well by now my consultant was Dr J. Varley, neurologist at the Children's hospital. While my family and me were at the hospital; "We are concerned about Lee. "Because from about the age of nine months he has had laughing attacks, he says he can have as many as six a day. "They begin with his eyes opening wide and he appears afraid."

This Dr. J. Varley would also be saying while still writing his information down. "They last a few seconds and suddenly he laughs, not a happy laugh which goes on for around 10-20 seconds. "Occasionally he has a temper after these episodes. "Lee can abort the turns by clenching his fists and he seems to dislike them." Dr J. Varley also then mentioned; "It is quite clear that Phenobarbitone reduced the number of episodes. But he has not had any for twelve months."

Also mentioned was "We have also noticed that occasionally after eating, lee has a red linear fl ush on the left side of his face. "The flush is about three quarters of an inch wide. It runs from the lower part of the ear to the left cheek bone by the side of his mouth. "Generally Lee is an active boy who enjoys outdoor play." My mum Kate then said.

Well unexpectedly "My impression is that lee's laughing episodes are an epileptic phenomenon and I have seen a boy with similar behaviour due to epilepsy – you will remember that he did well on Carbamazepine and I hope lee will do the same. Dr. J. Varley then said. Next "However, before starting this I would be grateful if lee could have another EEG here." then Dr J. Varley finished.

Well, on our next visit in the late 1970's, "Lee's EEG is normal, never the less as you know. I have suggested that he have Carbamazepine 100mg." Dr. J. Varley said. So now more medication!! This by taking diazepam in the morning and also at night.

We left the hospital and went back home to the Scott Arms. Next day just getting on and enjoying my life, wondering what the hell am I doing taking these tablets.

They are doing nothing for me and I do not have a health problem. My family regularly told me never let your misfortunes take over your life and never cry about them of which I do not ever do.

World Parks

Controlled Gardens

Whilst investigating so many places surrounding nature with enjoyment and conversation expanded amounts of gathered time has been spent going through places like Central Park educating viewable along so much the gardens stretch from North 110th Street to Central Park South inside Manhattan of New York gardens looking along to the back are much higher such as the Empire and also the World Trade Centre of with has been personally seen and of which has unbelievably large sky scrapers the Trade centre reached 107th floors to the top of the buildings this massive structured building became so high along with more to discuss in the minutes to come great fun.

The White House

Regulatory brings umpteen mounting viewable and enjoyably knowledgeable places unto interest reachable like gardens for going to observe places such as in the Kennedy gardens and more of which has become many umpteen the most successful places outside of the White House in which has seen visible on regular socialisations along from being invited personally for the White House Grounds to which are the oldest continually maintained landscape in the United States. One weekend during the spring and fall the White House South Grounds are open to the public. Visitors have the opportunity to see the two formal gardens, the Rose Garden near the West Wing and the Jacqueline Kennedy Garden near the East Wing as well as the Kitchen Garden which became established in 2009. Along with the gardens visitors can castigate many of the ornamental trees planted by former presidents and personally witnessed.

Buckingham Palace

Interestingly Buckingham Palace has served as the official London residence of the UK's sovereigns since 1837 and today is the administrative headquarters of the Monarch. Although in use for the many official events and receptions held by The Queen, the State Rooms at Buckingham Palace are open to visitors **every summer.**

Buckingham Palace has 775 rooms. These include 19 State rooms, 52 Royal and guest bedrooms, 188 staff bedrooms, 92 offices and 78 bathrooms. In measurements, the building is 108 metres long across the front, 120 metres deep (including the central quadrangle) and 24 metres high been to see as well interesting.

Along each line though interestingly produced is Buckingham Palace of which has served as the official London residence for the UK's sovereigns since 1837 and today is the administrative headquarters of the Monarch. Although in use for the many official events and receptions held by The Queen, the State Rooms at Buckingham Palace are open to visitors every summer.

Whilst along with everything Buckingham Palace has 775 rooms. These include 19 State rooms, 52 Royal and guest bedrooms, 188 staff bedrooms, 92 offices and 78 bathrooms. In measurements, the building is 108 metres long across the front, 120 metres deep (including the central quadrangle) and 24 metres high been to see as well interesting.

St James Park

Another observed has been St James's Park is at the heart of ceremonial London. It is the setting for spectacular pageants, like Trooping the Colour, and is surrounded by some of the country's most famous landmarks including Buckingham Palace, Clarence House, St James's Palace and Westminster.

But there is also another side to St James's Park; it is a tranquil place. Simply relax in a deckchair and watch the world go by. The flower beds and shrubberies are enjoyed by visitors all the year round.

St James's Park has been at the centre of the country's royal and ceremonial life for more than four hundred years. Royal ambitions and national events have shaped many of the features in the park.

Hyde Park

Set right in the heart of London, Hyde Park offers both world-class events and concerts together with plenty of quiet places to relax and unwind.

You can see the Diana, Princess of Wales Memorial Fountain, brave an open water swim in the Serpentine, or just admire the views across the lake from a waterside café.

Have a go at boating, tennis, horse riding, or join the many joggers, walkers and cyclists enjoying the open air.

Also explainable has been Hyde Park which has a long history as a site to protest, and still hosts rallies and marches today. Visit Speakers' Corner on a Sunday morning to hear people from all walks of life shares their views.

Hyde Park is one of London's eight Royal Parks and covers an area of 350 acres great for somebody to see.

Green Park

Although situated so close to St James's Park, The Green Park is quite different in character. It is more peaceful with mature trees and grassland and is surrounded by Constitution Hill, Piccadilly and the Broad Walk.

The Green Park was first recorded in 1554 as the place where a rebellion took place against the marriage of Mary I to Philip II of Spain. It was a famous duelling site until 1667 when Charles II bought an extra 40 acres and it became known as upper St James's Park.

The Green Park is a peaceful refuge for people living, working or visiting central London, and is particularly popular for sunbathing and picnics in fine weather. It is also popular as a healthy walking route to work for commuters. The paths are used extensively by joggers and runners must explain.

Red House Park

I will leave the medical side of the story for a minute and go onto talk more about the pleasures of my childhood. By now and having started infant school in 1975 on the Walsall Road of the Scott Arms. I was to start having reading and writing lessons along with learning mathematics. Then after and around school I was to play with class mates at Red House Park. This around the corner of the school in the Scott Arms of Birmingham. At the time being while I was also having loads of fun at home as well. My mates and me would all play together often running around the massive high hills. Or at other times going around and onto the big trees. Also enjoying many other things we would play games such as hide and seek whilst also maybe playing conkers against each other.

Another would also maybe playing soccer on the sports pitches around the park. At other times we would sometimes play by our homes maybe by our flats. Plus also behind the trees and down below the hills. My mum's fl at was on Hillside Road at the bottom of Red House Park. Then also just around the corner on Hilland Road was my Grandad George Grice's house. Who also lived at the Scott Arms.

Constantly mates and me would always be playing together.

While competing against each other in groups we had such a really good laugh on Red house Park. I would never stop and was constantly on the go all of the time. Now this part of my life was starting to build my confidence.

Often at around the age of seven I would be playing with my fort and army soldiers. These of which I had received for Christmas presents. Also there was the watching of television. Throughout the week, I would watch my favourite television programs. Some of these TV shows were great, such as Magic Roundabout, Knightrider (with Kit the car) I remember it well. Other television programs were like Rainbow (Bungle, Zippy, George, Jeffrey.)

Of course we also then had on the television. Mr Ben where he used to go on into a shop. Th en try diff erent clothes on. Also I watched Captain Pugwash. Another show on television was Worzal Gummidge on a Sunday. Whilst also my favourite cartoon show of which I still watch now and that was Scooby Doo. Along with these there were other television shows I remember. But the biggest of all must have been Winnie the Pooh. Which is one of the best-loved fi gures in British children's literature. Pooh was the creation of author A.A. Milne, who was inspired by the stuff ed toys of his son Christopher Robin. Pooh is a chubby stuff ed bear with a particular fondness for honey; his friends in the Hundred Acre Wood include Eeyore the sad donkey, Piglet the pig, and Tigger the bouncy tiger.

Also we had the Sweeney which ran from 2 January 1975 until 28 December 1978. At the start of the Sweeney television police drama shows. I loved the tune and the car going forward. When the tune began at the beginning of the Sweeney. I would always be getting up then starting to sing and dance.

Along with watching the television, I would still always be going back and forth constantly trying to do many other things. But still I had to put up with this one major problem.

These tingling stomach sensations! Tickling, tingling in my stomach like a tickling electronic shock! Still at the speed of a person's heart beat. Constantly I was trying to take no notice. Regularly I would still be enjoying myself at school and in the parks of Birmingham. Plus also it was fun reading my soccer shoot magazines and collecting my stickers for my soccer sticker book.

But by now, I still had to make continuous visits to doctors. Of which was starting to become very boring.

Always having to explain how I was getting on with medication. "Well, I do not seem to be getting very far with this tablet, "These tingling sensations seem to still be here,"

I would be saying to doctors and neurologists everywhere constantly in the hospital.

The tingling came on more and more it never seemed to ever end. Many times I was still tested with EEG tests, MRI and CAT scans but nothing would show up. What were these stomach sensations?

So constantly still on from the 1970's and into the early 1980's. At our home of Great Barr we still went thinking and trying to work out what was causing these tingling stomach problems.

Well I would still try to take no notice of things while taking my medication. Always to be enjoying myself in my hometown of Birmingham with mates. Seeing a friendly person every day really makes a person feel as though they are at home, of this I always found in Birmingham.

The White House

Now over in the States there are also including so many viewable and enjoyably interesting places of interest reached like gardens for going to observe places exploreable as in the Kennedy gardens and more of which has become many of the most successful places outside of the White House in which has become seen on regular invitations and invited personally the

White House Grounds are the oldest continually maintained landscape in the United States. One weekend during the spring and fall the White House South Grounds are open to the public. Visitors have the opportunity to see the two formal gardens, the Rose Garden near the West Wing and the Jacqueline Kennedy Garden near the East Wing as well as the Kitchen Garden which became established in 2009. Along with the gardens visitors can view many of the ornamental trees planted by former presidents and personally witnessed.

Washington DC.

Mail

Now the Mail reaches out viewable to see umpteen monuments rise majestically to the sky, surrounded by the stately U.S. Capitol Building at one end and the dignified Lincoln Memorial at the other, it's hard not to think of America's Mail in history. Explore the swath of land nicknamed "America's front yard" and you'll find inspiring monuments and memorials, museums and family fun that were just behind Capital Hill the US Senators building.

Central Park

Now this well certainly somewhere if not many seems of interest for anybody to go along and visit excitedly are the places with areas like Central Park in Manhattan of New York of that personally myself have visited reaching there on many occasions at which is held in Manhattan looking around in this little pretty park the size really of Red House Park come across both superb at which Red House is at the city of Birmingham very much so to which is nice and colourful plenty of flowers plus many trees centred right in the middle of the city come across really nice it was great for me to have seen the park regularly great have and joyful memories of the colourful gardens.

Whilst observing so many places involved with enjoyment and conversation expanded amounts of gathered time has been spent going through places like Central Park interestingly viewing so much the gardens stretch from North 110th Street to Central Park South inside Manhattan of New York gardens looking along to the back are much higher such as the Empire and also the World Trade Centre of with has been personally seen and of which has unbelievably large sky scrapers the Trade centre reached 107th floors to the top of the buildings this massive structured building became so high along with more to discuss in the minutes to come great fun.

Enjoyably so many parks have been visited and worked on with great success New York was interesting along with the Washington Mail soon and becoming involved were surrounded respectable places to memory like London where very interesting successful places became seen in and throughout gone as well as today plus surrounding the future.

Capital Hill

City

Golden Gate Bridge 2

Grand Canyon Rainbow

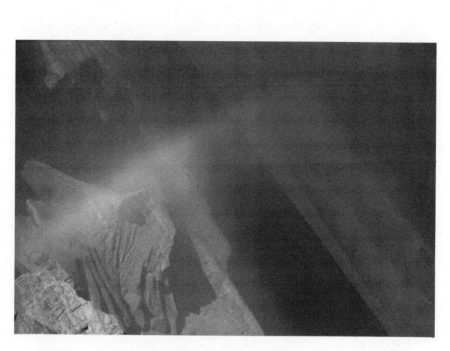

Grand Canyon Rainbow.jpg 2

Grand Canyon

Hawaii

Hawaii 2

Me outside White House

New York World Trade Centre

New York

Rivers

San Fransisco

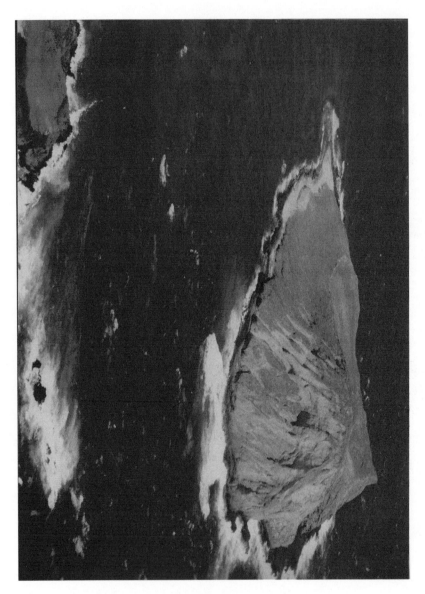

Sea Side US

Seattle helecopter 1 2005 from sky

World Trade Centre

Television companies

Beginning

Throughout the week, I would watch numerous channels whether British or numerous others around the world interesting brings in CBS News this channel of which is the news division of American television and radio service coming from New York along with ABC of whom The American Broadcasting Company (ABC) is an American television network. Created in 1943 from the former NBC Blue radio network, ABC is owned by The Walt Disney Company and is part of Disney-ABC Television Group . . .

With Happy Days, *Happy Days* was an American television sitcom that aired first-run from January 15, 1974, to September 24, 1984 on ABC More on with the television channel ABC on Charlie's Angles the show aired on ABC from 1976 to 1981 also in 1978-1991 on CBS you had Dallas which became a drama that revolves around the Ewings, a wealthy Texas family in the oil and cattle-ranching industries. Another show became Hawaii Five-O this was a police procedural drama series set in Hawaii that aired for twelve seasons from 1968 to 1980.

Back in England you could watch television programs such as Magic Roundabout or Knightrider (with Kit the car) I remember it well. Other television programs were like Rainbow (Bungle, Zippy, George, Jeffrey.) course we also then had on the television. Mr Ben where he used to go on into a shop. Then try different clothes on. Also I watched Captain Pugwash. Another show on television was Worzal Gummidge on a Sunday. Whilst also my favourite cartoon show of which I still watch now and that was Scooby Doo. Along with these there were other television shows I remember. But the biggest of all must have been Winnie the Pooh. Which is one of the best-loved figures in British children's literature. Pooh was the creation of author A.A. Milne, who was inspired by the stuffed toys of his son Christopher Robin. Pooh is a chubby stuffed bear with a particular fondness for honey; his friends in the Hundred Acre Wood include Eeyore the sad donkey, Piglet the pig, and Tigger the bouncy tiger.

Also we had the Sweeney which ran from 2 January 1975 until 28 December 1978. At the start of the Sweeney television police drama shows.

I loved the tune and the car going forward. When the tune began at the beginning of the Sweeney or Mash. I would always be getting up then starting to sing and dance.

Then on we went into the 1980's you had starting in 1983-1987 with NBC was the A-Team is an action adventure series about a fictional group of ex-United States Army Special Forces personnel who work as soldiers of fortune, coming ni regularly more comig along became a series.

Twentieth Century Fox Television (or TCFTV, stylized as 20th Century Fox Television) is the television production division of 20th Century Fox, and a production arm of the Fox Television Group one with many others produced became *M*A*S*H, Mash* is a 1972–1983 American television series developed by Larry Gelbart, adapted from the 1970 feature film produced by Fox Television.

Along with watching the television, I would still always be going back and forth constantly trying to do many other things. But still I had to put up with this one major problem.

These tingling stomach sensations! Tickling, tingling in my stomach like a tickling electronic shock! Still at the speed of a person's heart beat. Constantly I was trying to take no notice. Regularly I would still be enjoying myself at school and in the parks of Birmingham. Plus also it was fun reading my soccer shoot magazines and collecting my stickers for my soccer sticker book.

But by now, I still had to make continuous visits to doctors. Of which was starting to become very boring.

Always having to explain how I was getting on with medication. "Well, I do not seem to be getting very far with this tablet, "These tingling sensations seem to still be here," I would be saying to doctors and neurologists everywhere constantly in the hospital.

Th e tingling came on more and more it never seemed to ever end. Many times I was still tested with EEG tests, MRI and CAT scans but nothing would show up. What were these stomach sensations?

So constantly still on from the 1970's and into the early 1980's. At our home of Great Barr we still went thinking and trying to work out what was causing these tingling stomach problems.

Well I would still try to take no notice of things while taking my medication. Always to be enjoying myself in my hometown of Birmingham with mates. Seeing a friendly person every day really makes a person feel as though they are at home, of this I always found around the world.

Which team?

Next in the story, I go on to mention again the big subject's: School and Sports! At school between 1975 and 1982 bells would go off. Then it would be the end of a class lesson for playtime! In between lessons was good fun with my mates!

We were now all to become big soccer fans of West Midlands teams. That would mean you supported West Bromwich Albion, Birmingham City, Aston Villa or Wolverhampton Wonderers.

Also surrounding numerous other sports would and still do come along like American football involving the New York Giants or Boston Red Socks from Fenway Park of Massachusis out inside America

My first infant school named St Margaret's Infant School was just around the corner from Grandad George's house and our flat at the Scott Arms. Well in Great Barr, unfortunately for me though most people followed one team as I was to find out. While I was to eventually end up supporting West Bromwich Albion football club. All of my class mates would end up starting to support Aston Villa. As it was another part of the

Aston Villa supporter's area in and around American states like Los Angeles they have so much to see parks but with each state there are so many things to see or work in bit of difference might be Disney or Universal studios Birmingham. Texas you have many things but the biggest subect in that state shall probably always be where President J.F.Kennedy was shot on Elm Street in Dallas more to discuss later.

What should I do?

Why was I this Albion fan in Great Barr? Well this was due to all of my family coming from West Bromwich. Constantly when playing with my schoolmates. I had to perform as every West Bromwich Albion soccer player by myself. While doing this I should have received so many gold stars as awards from the headmaster. If I myself had been living just one minute up the Newton Road. Next to where mum was born by the Old Church I would have been living in West Bromwich with future which became in California around the brisk well-built mountains. going onto school with millions of Albion fans instead of Villa. Crazy I still often think to myself would it have been the same between the Giants and San Francisco 49rs which become much noticed whilst living in that later just off Oakland in San Francisco.

October 25th

Well on October 25th 1977, I went along to see the Albion for the first time ever. They played against Watford winning West Bromwich Albion 1-0 Watford.

After my first visit in 1977, something I will always this top class side in the West Midlands or at other times following Barcelona out in Spain. Well the Baggies that was the next goal I saw at the Albion. Extraordinarily it was to be a goal that the sports keepers like Tony Godden let in. Suddenly I would with different ideas probably this due to stress of seeing goals against or for the Albion. But also because many of my mates being Aston Villa fans missed out. Next day I tell you would they be playing me up about it at school or would it play back with the Albion scoring.

The game I personally remember most was seen in 1979, This was West Bromwich Albion playing against China XI at the Albion ground where we won Albion 4-0 China XI and more to discuss as we go along.

The West Bromwich Albion stadium is called the Hawthorns on the Birmingham Road in West Bromwich of the West Midlands in the United Kingdom. Many other games reach memory

Furthermore one memory I must mention in the story. This of which was to happen outside our Maisonette at the Scott Arms of Great Barr on 09th February 1980.

Suddenly my mate and me started playing soccer and I began impersonating one soccer player named Diego Maradona. To show my mate what a fantastic goal I had seem on the television. Well not the Albion players for once but he had been playing for Norwich City. "Hey Jase, watch this have just seen a great goal on the television." I shouted.

Then I threw the football into the air. When kicking the ball it flew into net "Goal!" it went straight through and into the net. Then did Jase and me run back home with our team celebrating with everybody me being the star similar to the way I would be celebrating on scoring a try whilst in the academy for Rugby for Handsworth Rugby club in the centre parts of Birmingham.

Well coming around Red House Park on the day after I had hit the ball into that net was unbelievable because when arriving back from St Margaret's Infant everybody was celebrating with me at school. Suddenly I started walking upstairs back into our flat. In shock!

Well, unexpectedly my mate Jason who I had been playing with at the time day of so much sport wondrously well his mum and dad were suddenly coming upstairs. At that time to our maisonette "Lee we will explain how good you are at shooting that was good." they said. Oh thanks! I could not believe it.

Soon they went upstairs to my mum's then I assume discussed all about what they had been told. My mum was very impressed with me all. I got a really good conversation of luckily interestingly first start with plenty more to come the start now began at looking into rugby plenty of ideas was said after about it. Soon I was to eventually find out it was Jason that had told his mum and dad t had been his brother going and passing the information on to his parents.

In a minute I will be bringing some more of my unexpected experiences all back into the story about my life then chat on about many amazing, exciting and unbelievable appearances. Which maybe is about visiting countries like Italy, Poland, Canada and the country I love America and much more success at University with personally listening to other people in and surrounding medical concerns with the government policies inside and out around the world

Now then one thing about me is that I cannot stop ever talking about my interests and experiences. Whatever the subject, maybe it will be to my daughter Natalie plus my mother or somebody else in my family. Regularly these are about medical subjects or countries and sports.

When talking about supporting the Baggies as fans call West Bromwich Albion. Often I hear "You have many great interests." Well the comment back is always "Yes, along with confidence it takes everything out of my mind." The funny thing is if I am quiet. Well everybody thinks that something has gone on. So I must talk about something interesting at some time or another otherwise everybody would leave the room but this can be due to concentration in University from Harvard in Boston or Wolverhampton studied at them both and bills involving Medicare or Medicaid along with the health service called the National Health Service.

So why do I never bring interest about things like soccer or different places around the world? It is just me and once a person has that personality. It will never change.

Th e thing that changes is education. What is this you may wonder? Well from what I have noticed listening is number one advancing ideas of success and helping others At the same time though this means when everybody is out of the room at Magda and my house. Then I can have my music or television on as loud as I want. Whether sports or Music!!! Great!!!

Well in 1980 on reaching the age of nine my dad Christopher and Grandad Geoff bought me my first soccer season ticket. So then off my Granddad Geoff and I went to watch regular matches. This going along supporting West Bromwich Albion around Great Britain. The big match however was and always will be West Bromwich Albion against Aston Villa for me. After having thirty-one school class-mates supporting Aston Villa. What else would you expect?

The first soccer player I was ever to worship was Cyril Regis. Having such an unbelievable right footed shot at goal!

He was fantastic and one of the first British black football players. Cyril played at the Albion for seven years scoring more than 100 goals for the Baggies. Also during his time with the Albion he played for the England International team on many occasions including the World Cup in Spain of 1982.

Barcelona

Real Madrid

Now having met the teams and him many times I was only nine years old when first meeting him. That was when my mum and dad took me into a big shopping store in the West Midlands.

Luckily I had a photograph taken with him. There were so many other people of which were waiting to meet him.

But luckily I was first in the line then after having the photograph he also signed my picture with him now becoming an adult meeting him and numerous other players has become untenably of great honour.

Well while still back at home in Birmingham or later San Francisco. Some more of my other favourite television programs would come on. The super special day would always be Saturday of which was made up of two different projects.

At the start of Saturday morning it was Tizwas. That television programme being my favourite show of the week. The show had Chris Tarrent, Sally James, Spit the dog and Bob Carolgees also with comedians such as Lenny Henry acting as Trevor MacDoughnut. This was something I would never miss constantly being excited while the program went on from 1974 to 1982.

At the same time I watched Postman Pat which was a British stop-motion animated children's television series first produced by Woodland Animations. It was aimed at preschool children, and concerns the adventures of Pat Clifton, a postman in the fictional village of Greendale (inspired by the real valley of Longsleddale in Cumbria). Postman Pat's fi rst 13-episode season was screened on BBC1 in 1981. John Cunliff e wrote the original treatment and scripts, and it was directed by animator Ivor Wood, who also worked on The Magic Roundabout, Paddington Bear, and Th e Herbs. Each episode followed the adventures of Pat Clifton, a friendly country postman, and his "black and white cat" Jess, as he delivers the post through the valley of Greendale. Although he initially concentrates on delivering his letters, he nearly always becomes distracted by a concern of one of the villagers and is usually relied upon to resolve their problems. Notable villagers include the postmistress: Mrs.Goggins, Alf Thompson: a farmer, and the local handyman and inventor, Ted Glen.

Whilst also as the 1980's came along the television shows to come on were shows like Minder and the Young Ones with Rik Mayall in and Adrian Edmondson. Strange, I was listening to an interview on Television by Rik Mayall from the Young Ones TV show in 2000. This after he had become seriously injured. When crashing a quad bike in 1998 near his home of Devon. Eventually when recovering from a coma after five days and coming out of hospital. Later saying he made a full recovery, he has been one of my all time favourite comedians. But he has since had two seizures, initially after being prescribed Phenytoin sodium, possibly due to not taking his medication, nothing else has been heard since.

Next after Tizwas it was then straight over to my Granddad Geoff's off licence in West Bromwich. Luckily for me it was "Lee we are now going off to the Albion." Grandad would say. Or maybe if lucky, it would also be more different soccer grounds in and around other parts of Great Britain. Then after the game my family and I would be back at home. Next watching the repeated soccer matches. That had been played throughout that day on BBC's Match of the Day added so along with BBC or Fox even ABC and NBS plus CBS and ITV so many channels emerging around the States and the United Kingdom available for the world.

Exploring but Still Stuck!!

Well while enjoying myself unfortunately I was still to be visiting hospitals. Mainly I would still be visiting the Children's hospitals around such plaqces as Los Angeles or in Birmingham and seeing Dr J.D.Varley. This now along with many other neurologists because everybody was still becoming confused as to what was causing all of my problems. Eventually while everybody still studied my 16 medical situation. Doctors would put me onto many other forms of medication. The name of one tablet was and still is called Sodium Valporate (Epilm). This of which controls convulsions (fits or seizures). On reducing the activity in the brain with some forms of epilepsy.

Oh no, what is going on! And also what would I soon be starting to think things about hospitals while having a lot of fun outside! But by now I had a lot on my mind in and out of school.

Funny though, there was still to be even more excitement outside school and defiantly hospitals. One super story was my exciting time on holiday with my school out into Belgium and Holland. There was a great story of which I will explain. This was concerning me and my mate. Well while out on this tour by ferry with many of St Margaret's Infant School around Europe. My mate and me were walking around over the roads in Belgium.

At the time while still on this vacation with many of our other school classmates.

Suddenly, though after playing on the go-carts mates and me both started going along passed a stadium. Whilst there I had a fast run across the parks. Well when he came back out we both ended up laughing! Somehow I did not get into any trouble. Recently, "As I remember lee we were only playing around." Steve mentioned. Who I saw a few years ago back in Birmingham.

Now then around all of that must mention about the many different tours I did as a child with my family around the world.

Well to start off with as a little boy. Mum, dad and me would regularly be going on holiday. Mum and dad would be sun bathing and traveling around I would also be on the beach making sand castles.

At other times I would be with my Granddad George who still lived just around the corner from us on Highland Road at the Scott Arms of Great Bar in Birmingham.

Well Granddad George would regularly take me to his parties in Lakeside Holiday Park at Burnham on sea. One day on my many trips with him well this one occasion it was really funny. This was when I acted a bit of a sports star comedian on one of my many trips there with Grandad.

This was when doing some photography of the sportsmen. It was so funny because it made him laugh and gave him the concentration the next day.

Along with this my family and I regularly went off on holiday to Cornwall and Devon. Mind you something very funny happened on one occasion. This was when dad put a hat on mums head it was worded Albion and she said "Thanks!! Explaining how much she supported the Albion herself. Well it went straight onto my mum's head just as we reached Lands End of Cornwall. Around our visits to the seaside of England we all went around other places such as Corfu, Spain to Barcelona and Ibiza.

Now back to writing about my school years in vision. We'll probably the one and only thing I used to like was going back and forth Albion home and away shirts great in and outside of St Margaret's Infant school of Great Barr. That was so much fun for me people would be laughing with me more than they were supporting West Bromwich Albion.

Regularly: "Why did I at school to wear Albion shirts mum?" I have asked. Well: "Lee because you were the top Albion fan in Great Barr she regularly tells me.

Now outside of school in Central or Red House Park I would still just be getting fed up of having to go back and forth into hospitals. By now starting to reach high school I could not believe my medical records were becoming so big. "Sorry Lee, we still cannot work out what is causing these giggling stomach feelings." Now not only would I have this red rash on the side of my left cheek but I was now starting to go red in the face with frustration. I just had to spend a lot of my time there. This to see if the doctors could work out what these irritating stomach sensations were. Just gritting my teeth and concentrating in my mind. Regularly thinking about my other pleasures such as watching the Albion and my dreams in life to stop the frustration. Thinking about it now I did well having to control all these problems. This was and still is a very big achievement of which I constantly think about. "Because it was dame hard but confidence kept me going!" Regularly I am still telling people when having to visit and the other being all withed became support groups for hospitals around London or America along with many so many more involving the life.

Now then back to enjoyment in my life of the subject around the world. This could be in either reading or writing about sports and politics whilst great hopes at following as many teaching schools and hospitals around the world will talk later about the National Health Service and other polies like Medicare and Medicaid both of which became set up by Senator Edward Kennedy in 1971.

Up to the age of six and looking into the history of football with my personal soccer team they have reached so many successful times last of the two legged road to wining became West Ham 2 – 1 West Brom and then back at the Hawthorns the score was West Brom 4 – 1 making the final score West Brom 5 – 3 West Ham and winning trophies because you have the most followed in Britain and that is the F.A.Cup of which the Albion have won five times first in 19 plus 1931 coming back in 1935 they lost but again rolled in for 1954 winning beating Sheffield Wednesday 3 – 2.

- Bringing out the very successful team in the 1960's many trophies were won like the league cup against West Ham in the last two legged matches just mentioned ____ they next went along into the first league cup final but losing 3 – 2 to Queens Park Rangers after being in front two nil and then the one still followed most is the 1968 FA Cup Final where Jeff Astle scored at Wembley himself though losing his life to something still very much being studied
- After that match the Albion next went along again to play Manchester City but after going 1 – 0 up they lost 2 – 1 of that soccer group from up north soon though the Albion went through a few seasons of winning nothing apart from the third in the league league and UAFA Cup but even though not winning due to having a strong team they lost in the quarter final to ____ whilst having finished third in the league table many well played matches brought us into having this amazing season.

Two years of great interest in 1978 – 1979 became when the Albion played in the first round [C] Galatasaray1–3 (A), 3–1 (H) next onto the Second round [image] Braga0–2 (A), 1–0 (H) next the Third round [image] Valencia1–1 (A), 2–0 (H) but losing in the Quarter-finals to [image] Red Star Belgrade1–0 (A), 1–1 (H).

Back to me following them in sports because at the 1981-82 season the baggies went into two Semi-Finals but lost in both. On the one occasion though, I went into school with a massive smile on my face. This was because the Albion had beaten Aston Villa at Villa Park. In the Quarter Finals of the League Cup (Formally at the time the Milk Cup) that put us into the Semi-Final of the competition. Aston Villa 0—1 West Bromwich Albion.

Well, suddenly in the game Gary Owen crossed the ball and Derek Statham slid in to put the ball under Jimmy Rimmer and into the net, oh did we all go wild!!! Remember all very well, standing in the Trinity road end at Villa Park. This on January 20th 1982. But the unfortunate thing was that after the pleasure of beating the Villa. The Albion went on to loose in the Semi-finals. The first match was a two-legged semi-final against Tottenham Hotspur. The first being at the Hawthorns: West Bromwich Albion 0-0 Tottenham Hotspur. Next in the second leg it was then Tottenham 1—0 West Bromwich Albion at White Hart Lane in London. Next the other heart breaking game was being just after I reached the age of eleven.

I had been running around at home when suddenly from school having received an award for good play. Well this meant I had to go down to the next game again with a West Brom shirt on well the game was on Saturday, April 3rd 1982, played at Highbury in London. That being home of Arsenal football club. The match was between the Albion and Queens Park Rangers. All of us Albion fans thought it would be easy. Only for us to lose from Queens Park Rangers 1-0 West Bromwich Albion to the most ridiculous goal you could ever imagine.

Many interests have been inside and around my life which keeps your mind active different sports and stories read good socialisation good exercise and eventually your interests shall reach more keeping the mind active for new adventures to reach out for the future.

By now still at school in the 1980's, we had music groups playing "Out and loud!" around class like Duran Duran that started ni 1979 from my home city of Birmingham with "Girls on fi lm!" "Rio!" then songs like "Notorious!" that went to Number 2 in the U.S.A. Then other hits recently like "Red Carpet Massacre!". You also had Roxy Music from up north by then the group had hits like "Virginia Plain!" "Love is the drug!" "Angle Eyes!" and my favourite song named "Th e same Old Scene!" in 1982 the last album became "Avalon!" This album reached number one in the UK album charts

Top Groups would suddenly arrive into the world you had Bon Jovi and Guns N Roses both personal favourites Axl Rose and Slash top stars of Guns N Roses along the way now even though I had walked into school celebrating about that win against the Villa.

Unluckily in the middle of the 1980's this was soon to be a terrible time for us Baggies fans. Eventually in school on reaching the age of eleven I was now finally wearing the school suite! But now it was time to move on and also for the last School class picture at St Margaret's Infant School. Of course all of my school mates were there. I was on the photograph wearing a 1982 World Cup in Spain jumper on but all of my mates were standing there in Aston Villa shirts, typical. Me aged eleven at St Margaret's. Eventually in 1982, my family and I moved home from our flat on Hillside Road. This time to a house on the Howard Road luckily still only one minute across the other side of Red House or later times for me to be in Central Park of New York.

Around the moving and school I had many games. For my twelfth birthday of 27ᵗʰ April 1983, I had a little Skay Electric sports car. Plus other things like a new Albion home and away shirt. On Tuesday 1ˢᵗ May of 1983, was playing with my electric Grandstand Mini-Munchman. These while also having my Subuteo game. Where, I played with little plastic toy Soccer players on a small cotton soccer pitch.

At this time, I was to also to have my first ever riding bike. The bike was a Rally Commando. So off I would go on the bike having a lot of fun. Going to my school "Zooming!" up and down hills and around the Red House parks. But somehow I would constantly still be getting frustrated. Due to the giggling that was still causing my voice tone to rise dramatically.

Later on in 1983, after starting Dartmouth High School I was still to be just as stupid as when living in my flat on Hillside Road. Because while in a music lesson with mates. On grabbing a puma pump, "Hey everybody, catch this!!" I shouted. Well on whacking the trainer top notch.

Instead of somebody if not everybody going to catch the puma pump. What did they do as it flew through the air?

Well, everybody ducked down and it went "Smash!" straight through the school. Great timing, because who was walking passed the hallway as all of this happened?

Could not believe my luck, it was our school headmaster Mr Manchin. "Who put this down the hallway?" he shouted. Of cause everybody turned around looking at me. Well, who was the goalkeeper!" he then said. After all of that I'd got told off and had to pay £2.00.

Of cause around all of that I would constantly still be enjoying myself. At dinner times in school I would be playing table tennis in Red House. While still having fun with mates in and around Black Country. All still while having the same tests in hospital. These tests would be: EEG plus also MRI, CAT and PET scans.

What tests are there?

Medical Tests:

There are so many forms of tests along with surgery you have the EEG tests where metal needles are inserted into your head on one occasion my skull was brought back plus another became fifty inserted my head casing a few seizures whilst these little needles were into my head like needles felling like blood tests into your arm recently in 2016.

The MRI is another form of test where you go into a tube and become scanned to make sure as to where the damage is from you brain is, The CAT Scan is extraordinarily strained because you are put nitro a box and become twirled around whilst holding a button until holding some form of epileptic seizure.

Well your neurologist may ask you to have some tests to get extra information about the seizures. The tests are usually done by a technician (a professor that is trained to do them). the results from the tests are then passed back to the neurologist to see what they show. The results may indicate that you have epilepsy and may also say why you have epilepsy.

There are many different causes of seizures and some other conditions can easily be mistaken for epilepsy.

Although seizures with different causes may look similar to epileptic seizures, there are often subtle differences which help your doctor to make the correct diagnosis. There are a number of tests that can help rule out other causes.

Blood tests

To do a blood test, a sample of blood is taken, usually from your arm, with a syringe. The sample is used to check your general health. The test is also used to rule out other possible causes of the seizures, such as low blood sugar levels or diabetes had many Electrocardiogram (ECG)

An ECG is used to record the electrical activity of the heart. This is done by sticking electrodes (a bit like plasters) to the arms, legs and chest. These electrodes pick up the electrical signals from the heart.

Because an ECG does not give out electrical signals, having one doesn't hurt. An ECG can help to rule out the seizure being caused by the way the heart is working Both these tests feel the same as inserting needles into your head and like neuro surgery Tests to help diagnose epilepsy.

No test can say for certain whether you do or do not have epilepsy. But when the information from the tests is added to the other information about what happens during the seizures, this builds up a clearer picture of what happened. This may help with the diagnosis and when choosing treatment.

Electroencephalogram (EEG)

An electroencephalogram (EEG) is a recording of brain activity of which has been something undertaken by me on an unbelievable amount of times and certainly in some shocking ways for instance let us talk soon.

Well then during the test, small sensors are plus have been attached to the scalp to pick up the electrical signals produced when brain cells send messages to each other electrically activity has certainly gone through me after having needles inserted

These signals are recorded by a machine and are looked at by a doctor later to see which certainly became unusual but became needed for any success in finding out as for what should become claimed for causing medical problems like mine.

The EEG procedure is usually carried out by a highly trained specialist called a clinical neurophysiologist during needed appearances whilst sometimes visiting people can sometimes be made long so as to make longer tests enabling success in coming in and from the hospital.

Interestingly an EEG can be used to help diagnose and monitor a number of conditions affecting the brain mine is concerning what became found out in being this Non-Malignant tumor plus only the size of some pen dot as mentioned.

It may help identify the cause of certain symptoms – such as seizures (fits) or memory problems – or find out more about a condition you've already been diagnosed with.

The main use of an EEG is to detect and investigate epilepsy, a condition that causes repeated seizures. An EEG will help your doctor identify the type of epilepsy you have, what may be triggering your seizures, and how best to treat you.

Less often, an EEG may be used to investigate other problems, such as dementia, head injuries, brain tumours, encephalitis (brain inflammation) and sleep disorders, such as obstructive sleep apnoea.

Your appointment letter will mention anything you need to do to prepare for the test but obviously even though having gone to the unfortunately letter receiving in England often becomes for all very poor as the health service in the country has very little in money

Unless told otherwise, you can usually eat and drink beforehand and continue to take all your normal medication thing is though hospital food really does taste out of date on receiving and eating any in vacations in hospital buildings.

To help the sensors stick to your scalp more easily, you should make sure your hair is clean and dry before arriving for your appointment and avoid using products such as hair gel and wax once having the electrodes taken out though you feel as though you have had real glue put into your hair as it takes forever to get out again.

You might want to bring a hairbrush or comb with you as your hair may be a bit messy when the test is finished. Some people bring a hat to cover their hair until they can wash it at home afterwards joke because whether washing or something else doing all really has achieved extraordinary results like supposedly not having epilepsy any more an explanation has bene given to me by Professor Rickards of the Queen Elizabeth hospital

How an EEG is carried out

There are several different ways an EEG recording can be taken. The clinical neurophysiologist will explain the procedure to you and can answer any questions you have. You'll also be asked whether you give permission (consent) for the various parts of the test to be carried out.

Then before the test starts, your scalp will be cleaned and about 20 small sensors called electrodes will be attached using a special glue or paste. These are connected by wires to an EEG recording machine.

Routine EEG recordings usually take 20 to 40 minutes, although a typical appointment will last about an hour, including some preparation time at the beginning and some time at the end. Other types of EEG recording may take longer.

There are different forms of these a routine EEG recording lasts for about 20 to 40 minutes personally though due to being and occasionally staying in hospital times and more have been quite longer at neurologists plus everybody studying this condition which even though having confidence and determination as put really brings good results

Whilst also going on during the test, you'll be asked to rest quietly and open or close your eyes from time to time. In most cases, you'll also be asked to breathe in and out deeply (known as hyperventilation) for a few minutes.

At the end of the procedure a flashing light may be placed nearby to see if this affects your brain activity.

Another form is the sleeping EEG which becomes carried out while you're asleep. It may be used if a routine EEG doesn't give enough information, or to test for sleep disorders.

In some cases, you may be asked to stay awake the night before the test to help ensure you can sleep while it's carried out. This is called a sleep-deprived EEG of cause which certainly became the decision for serious tests whilst having electrodes inserted inside my skull.

Others known about are ambulatory EEG tests where brain activity is recorded throughout the day and night over a period of one or more days. The electrodes will be attached to a small portable EEG recorder that can be clipped on to your clothing.

So many but this can continue with most of your normal daily activities while the recording is being taken, although you'll need to avoid getting the equipment wet.

Video telemetry

More of these should be used in Video telemetry, also known as video EEG, is a special type of EEG where you're filmed while a recording is taken. This can help provide more information about your brain activity also something that can often bring results but vidio recorded which arrive something experienced became made causing this personal epileptic seizure in Sandwell Council with no or success for people concerning them.

The test is usually carried out over a few days while staying in a purpose-built hospital suite timing EEG signals which are transmitted wirelessly to a computer the video is also recorded by the computer and kept under regular surveillance by trained staff which on person occasions have been superb with me.

When the test is finished, the electrodes will be removed and your scalp will be cleaned. Your hair will probably still be a bit sticky and messy afterwards, so you may want to wash it when you get home something just mentioned can something of more benefit be introduced for everybody of need to it.

Another is that people can usually go home soon after the test is finished and can return to your normal activities. We might feel tired after the test, particularly if you had a sleep or sleep-deprived EEG, so you may want someone to pick you up from hospital.

Unfortunately, must mention something though due to poor rated working results took forever to be organized enabling something to come after late December You won't normally get your results on the same day. The recordings will need to be analyzed first and will be sent to the doctor who requested the test. They can discuss the results with you a few days or weeks later eventually though everything became discussed with me some few months after the tests though some results did come but in conversation very misjudge able because of being told epilepsy has become something of which no suffering arrives is that true well.

The EEG procedure is painless, comfortable and generally very safe. No electricity is put into your body while it's carried out. Apart from having messy hair and possibly feeling a bit tired, you won't normally experience any after effects nothing like scars from the tests like me in the late 1980 years.

However, you may feel lightheaded and notice a tingling in your lips and fingers for a few minutes during the hyperventilation part of the test. Some people develop a mild rash where the electrodes were attached.

There's a very small risk you could have a seizure while the test is carried out, but you'll be closely monitored and help will be on hand in case this happens all of which seems to be involved with me but outside plus around there has been plenty of personal success being left to go back home on that resent occasion you press this button which brings some signal up enabling those supposed results to arrive on returning back to hospital to discuss everything.

Regularly if not always decisions concerning health objectives will and must be able to support one plus all to live more than happy lives with or without perfect health situations personality along with confidence though shall really enable one and every to bring more success plus happiness into life

Often if not always by helping people from the medical services unbelievable amounts should improve along with curing any if not all concerns due to reasons of being in hospital often success will arrive in plenty and throughout everything for more than subjectives from one and all.

More to come is that these metal needled tests can usually show if someone is having a seizure at the time of the inquests but it can't show what happens in the person's brain at any other time. So even though your test results might not show any unusual activity it does not rule out having epilepsy. Some types of epilepsy are very difficult to identify with an EEG test. Some people who do not have epilepsy can sometimes have irregular activity on their EEG. But a result where there is irregular activity does not necessarily mean that the person has epilepsy in and throughout life for the world but another was to come soon and needles oh yes you wait.

Sleep-deprived EEG

For some people there is more chance of irregular brain activity happening when they are tired or when they are going to sleep. If this is the case for you, having a sleep deprived EEG might help get a more useful reading. This test is done in the same way as a normal EEG but you sleep during the test. To help you sleep, you may be asked to stay awake some, or all, of the night before. In some cases you may be given a mild sedative to help you get to sleep.

Ambulatory EEG

An ambulatory EEG works in the same way as a normal EEG but is portable. It is a small machine that is worn on a belt around your waist. Because it is portable you can move around and carry on with your normal day-to-day routine while the recording happens.

This type of EEG allows brain activity to be recorded for several hours, days or weeks. Because the brain activity is recorded for longer, there is more chance of a seizure being recorded on the EEG than during the normal 30 minute test.

Video telemetry

Video telemetry testing happens in hospital, usually over a couple of days. During your stay you have your own room. In the room, often mounted on the wall, there is a video camera that records what you are doing. At the same time you will wear a portable EEG so that you are able to move around your room. Being videoed whilst wearing an EEG means that if you have a seizure your doctor can compare the electrical activity of your brain with what is happening to your body.

The results can help identify what types of seizure you are having, and the most appropriate way of treating them.

Brain scans

Brain scans can be used to help find the cause of someone's seizures. The scans produce pictures of the brain which might show a physical cause for epilepsy, such as scarring on the brain. But for many people a brain scan does not show up a cause for their seizures, and even if nothing unusual is seen, the person may still have epilepsy.

The two common types of brain scan are Magnetic Resonance Imaging and Computerised Axial Tomography.

(MRI scan)

Experienceing an Magnetic resonance imaging or MRI Scan really makes concentration and ideas powerful but all that happenes is you or somebody in need of the test shall be put onto some metal bed with tubing circled around the machine and then when everything begins the panelled bed of which you are put on goes into this tube whilst medical profesionals scan over and into the brain on computer screen this was of which has been used by medical workers on me on numerous occasions and the most importand one came along the day of the operation ni April 17 the scan was made and then on that day after the scan next time arrived for surgery.

An MRI scan uses strong magnetic fi elds to take images of the brain. Because of the magnetic fi elds, metal objects in or near the machine can aff ect, or be aff ected by, the machine. Before having an MRI scan you will need to remove any metal objects such as jewellery, hearing aids, coins or keys.

If you have a heart pacemaker or any surgical implant that contains metal you may not be able to have an MRI scan.

What happens during an MRI scan?

Th e scanner makes a loud noise so before it starts you will be given earplugs to wear. You will also be given a buzzer to hold—you can use the buzzer to let the technician know if you are feeling uncomfortable or unwell during the scan. Th e technician is usually on the other side of a window in another room during the scan, but an intercom means you can talk to them. Th ere is also usually a mirror inside the scanner so you can see the technician during the scan. You may be able to have someone in the room with you during the scan.

During the scan you will lie on a platform which slides backwards into the scanner. When having an MRI scan to help diagnose epilepsy the scan usually takes about 30 minutes. Lying still during the scan is important so that the machine can take a clear image.

An MRI scan is usually a series of short scans with breaks in between rather than one long scan. Between each short scan the technician might use the intercom to check that you are comfortable.

Computerised axial tomography (CT or CAT scan)

CT scans use X-rays to take images of the brain. CT scans are not suitable if you are pregnant because the X-rays could affect an unborn baby. During a CT scan you lie on a couch which slides into the scanner.

Confirmed

Well around all of these different medical tests everything still steamed in my head. This from the fact that doctors had no way and I had little way of controlling these tingling stomach sensations. Maybe it was a neurological problem but were these nerve cells in my stomach connecting to some part of my brain. Who knows!!

Doctors would go back and forth: "We think it could be epilepsy but we are not sure." all saying and stating different things. By now I had been plastered with this Sodium Valporate 600mg of a morning and 1000mg at night.

I would, constantly have to be repeating everything. This as to what was going on about sudden jumping in the night. Whilst also all concerning these giggling sensations in my stomach. Plus also a red rash of which I was getting on the left side of my face. Of course "We will have to wait for the EEG results!" neurologists and doctors would constantly be saying to me.

But suddenly in 1986, at the age of fi fteen horror!! Because everything was confi rmed to me. At the Queen Aston Univercity at King Edward Vi House, 1 Aston Street Eastside, Birmingham B4 7ET. "We are sorry Lee, the EEG test results have just come through. "You are having nighttime's grand mal Epileptic seizures!" doctors told me. This was terrible news!! So now I had epilepsy while also still getting these tingling sensations. What was all of this?

I had started to suff er tiredness due to the medication. Plus occasional brief episodes of dizziness of which was really making my life fun!!

Well what could I say do or think? Still at the Children's Hospital seeing Dr J.D. Varley. But now I had also started seeing another neurologist named Dr. Tim Betts. Who worked at Aston Univercity in King Edward

Vi House, Aston Street Eastside of Birmingham. In the West Midlands of the United Kingdom.

Somehow I was starting to have around six tonic-clonic seizures whilst asleep a month. Th ese of which I knew nothing about because I would be jumping in and out while sleeping. It was all quite confusing, so wondering what these forms of seizures were we had a chat with Dr J.D. Varley and Dr Tim Betts both in Birmingham.

They both told us all about different forms of epileptic seizures. "Tonic Clonic seizures and all the ones of which Lee is suffering with at night. "These are generalised seizures involving the whole brain. "It is the seizure type most people think of when they think of epilepsy. "Some people may experience an 'aura' such as a feeling of deja vu, a strange feeling in the stomach or a strange taste or smell, just before the seizure begins. "Th e aura itself is a simple partial seizure." Dr J Varley and Dr Tim Betts stated.

Well eventually my family and I were to leave the Children's hospital of Ladywood. Next in the middle of 1986 it was time for regular tests and conversations about the epilepsy with neurologists. All at the Queen Elizabeth Hospital in Edgbaston and now also Aston University of which are both in Birmingham.

I often visited Dr Tim Betts at the neurology department regularly as the epilepsy went on every day. Starting with what had sounded like simple partial attacks. With these tonic clonic seizures at night that were coming from the left temporal lobe of my brain.

The tonic clonic seizures increased and became more frequent, so next I was put onto the tablet named lamotrigine.

Pocket Money

Well, even though I had this sudden shock of epilepsy I still had good fun with mates as I went on everyday at Dartmouth High School. Everything was to be hard work but at the same time I made my school years a lot of fun. Because constantly as much as I studied. I was still one of the back row comedians in class. I would work hard in the English, Maths, Science and P.E. lessons. But sometimes in class I would be chucking paper direct at my teacher. Crack on! I thought. "Good shot, Lee!" my mates would say. Then "Who threw that!" the teacher shouted. Finding out it was me well then I would have to walk out. This to the front and apologise to my tutor and the class.

Eventually because of me throwing paper more than once, it was ruler time. "Whack!" across the hand and also sometimes I was to stand at the front of the class. Or even outside the room. I was still to eventually do well achieving many things. Because in my third year of school education. I started playing rugby in and outside of the school lessons. In sports lessons I would play for Churchill. While at other times playing for Dartmouth High School around Walsall and Birmingham. Throughout this at school my tutor Les Cusworth. Who played rugby for Leicester and England found me a very good athlete and <u>Rugby player.</u>

So off I went onto trial in rugby for a local West Midlands side named Hansworth.

Outside of that one good story was when going along to school with my Big D Bag. Or should I say: Big Dick bag, as my mates would call me. This bag was unbelievably a free present from my Grandad Geoff. He got it free from the Big D peanuts company. If anything cost my Grandad Geoff money he always made sure he got something back for it. I remember when I was a little boy, especially concerning my pocket money. I would go around to his off—licence and when asking him if I could have some sweets. Well "Yes you can Lee, have ten pence worth." So I got the sweets and put them into a paper bag. But suddenly "Lee, don't forget to put the ten pence in the till for your sweets." Grandad Geoff would say. On another occasion as I reached my late twenties. We were on our way up to the Albion soccer ground. We went past a side street store for hot dogs and burgers. Suddenly, "lee can you get me a burger, "Here is the pound to pay for the hamburger." But then of cause: "Lee, can I have the 1 pence change please." he said. I was laughing in shock it was crazy, because the burger cost 99 pence. It was unbelievable. But something though and that was even though he was stingy with money. Well he really cared and was always there to give me any help or advice about things.

Why Me!

Still fun at school some of these were as mentioned, that I'm a huge fan of Roxy Music, collecting all of their albums and singles. In the year of 2005, I had the fantastic honour of meeting three of the group. They were Phil Manzanera the guitar player, Paul Thompson the drummer and Andy Mackay the saxophone player only Bryan Ferry of the group to meet all from Roxy Music. This had been one amazing dream. Along with two other groups that will be mentioned. Another interesting thing was in 1985. I had been watching the Live Aid concert show at London. There were 1.4 billion television viewers worldwide glued watching this on the T.V screen. At the time of watching this I was living in another area of Birmingham named Sutton Coldfield. This was just down the road from Great Barr and just down the road from my school at the Scott Arms. This day with Live Aid on the television it was really funny. Soon Bryan Ferry came onto the television I pressed the recording button straight away on the recorder to tape him singing four songs. He was to sing three songs from his new Boys and Girls album; "Sensation, Boys and Girls, Slave to love", then to finish his part of the show, "Jealous Guy," which was the number one hit single from Roxy Music in 1981. Eventually of course, as many others around the world, (If not already there at Wembley,) just sang like myself all hearing loud and clear over their televisions and radios. This when suddenly all of the concert pop stars came out together at 21.56 to finish the concert by singing the song, "We are the World!" While the story caries on the main thing I write about. This is that I have so many joyful memories of school and when living in Birmingham. Along with music and soccer, another of my many interests would be collecting soccer programs.

I always went to second hand soccer program shops now having millions. Many of these shops were in Birmingham and West Bromwich. By then and looking now in my folders there are many of the F.A. Cup Final, League Cup and West Bromwich Albion programs. The soccer programs of Albion I have go back in many years gone past to around 1943. Many are worth a large amount of money now. Well now still I think in shock as I write in the story.

This about all that was to come. Even now in 2010, I get the memories inside my head. Th is of how have experienced so much. With thoughts of what could have often been the causes to have tingling sensations and this form of epilepsy in the years gone by. Will people ever understand how a person suffers inside? I have suffered dramatically hundreds of times daily. Why should people have to suffer? Just thought would it never stop. Psychologically your brain can play tricks with your mind. But luckily I was able to control mine.

How I wanted to scream and shout out. Why me! Why me! Everybody gets upset. But confidence and determination that would always enable me to live many unbelievable years to come.

CHAPTER TWO

NEW ADVENTURES

Change of area

Well on Friday 27th March 1987, while still at Dartmouth High School in Birmingham. I moved up with my mum up North still in the West. Regularly throughout school I was to have fourteen or more subject report assessments each year. Some of these were in Art, Creative Skills, Drama, English, Geography and Home Economics. Along with these I was to also study Languages, Life Skills, Mathematics, Music, Physical Education, Religious Education and also Sciences. Eventually after my exams I passed 4' O levels in English, Maths, Science and Geography. Then after having taken the exams my School education years in Birmingham were to finish. Still unfortunately though throughout my school years of Birmingham along with also having moved to Staff ord. I had to make regular visits to the Queen Elizabeth Hospital in Edgbaston of Birmingham. At the same time I was to now have a new General Practitioner name was Dr.J.P.Hannigan in Staff ord.

By now living in this new area of the West Midlands I would still be constantly saying to myself. "What are these dame giggling, tingling sensations in my stomach. "Regularly also thinking could this form of epilepsy ever be controlled."

Well eventually with more studying by doctors and neurologists. I was to fi nd out what was causing these seizures along with the giggling sensations in my stomach.

Aura

Eventually the giggling sensation would now have to be constantly explained and studied at hospitals. Somehow this was a kind of tingly stomach sensation. Unfortunately, there seemed to be no understanding. As to what was causing these tickly and tingling sensations. Next in this story, I go on to writing about how I would constantly be describing the giggling. "They are like a kind of tingling in the centre nerve of my stomach. "If you count to ten it is as if they are like the speed of your heartbeat." I would be saying.

So these evil things would start dramatically one, two, three, four, five, six, seven, eight, nine and ten. Suddenly the tingling sensation went a lot stronger in the centre of my chest. Then my voice tone would suddenly rise to a much higher level. I explained they were like somebody going "Boo!!" and making you jump out of your skin. Another way to explain this strangely enough was "That it is like a person having butterflies in their stomach" my mum would actually also explain to hospitals.

Well after the studying by Dr Patterson, plus me having visited Hallam hospital. I was next to move on and explain all of this again to many other hospitals.

Hallem Hospital

Children Hospital

Firstly, I was going on into the Children's hospital of Ladywood in Birmingham. But still not understanding I was to still be having to constantly repeat myself again and again with Doctors and neurologists.

"Doctor, Doctor, I am getting this tingling sensation in my stomach. "It is like a heart beat where it tingles in my stomach. "Like a kind of sensation when you jump out of your skin." I would again say.

Often I would have these tickling feelings in my stomach at the hospital. While at other times the giggling would be at school or somewhere else in Birmingham. When these ticking and tingling sensations started in the centre of my stomach. Somehow it would suddenly make my tone of voice increase. Sometimes "I felt so stupid constantly they were making me sound like a little girl!" I would often be saying to my mum and doctors.

Well by now my consultant was Dr J. Varley, neurologist at the Children's hospital. While my family and me were at the hospital; "We are concerned about Lee. "Because from about the age of nine months he has had laughing attacks, he says he can have as many as six a day. "They begin with his eyes opening wide and he appears afraid."

This Dr. J. Varley would also be saying while still writing his information down. "They last a few seconds and suddenly he laughs, not a happy laugh which goes on for around 10-20 seconds. "Occasionally he has a temper after these episodes. "Lee can abort the turns by clenching his fists and he seems to dislike them." Dr J. Varley also then mentioned; "It is quite clear that Phenobarbitone reduced the number of episodes. But he has not had any for twelve months."

Also mentioned was "We have also noticed that occasionally after eating, lee has a red linear flush on the left side of his face. "The flush is about three quarters of an inch wide. It runs from the lower part of the ear to the left cheek bone by the side of his mouth. "Generally Lee is an active boy who enjoys outdoor play." My mum Kate then said. Well unexpectedly "My impression is that lee's laughing episodes are an epileptic phenomenon and I have seen a boy with similar behaviour due to epilepsy – you will remember that he did well on Carbamazepine and I hope lee will do the same. Dr. J. Varley then said. Next "However, before starting this I would be grateful if lee could have another EEG here." then Dr J. Varley finished.

Tension and Anxiety

I was recently, talking to some neurologists and doctors. Where we discussed something of which I found quite interesting. People with tonic clonic seizures may or may not experience a warning. Where some people experience a sensation called an aura before a seizure starts. The aura may occur far enough in advance to give people time to lie down and prevent injury from falling. The type of aura experienced varies from person to person, as auras are in fact a simple partial seizure, for example: a change in body temperature, a feeling of tension or anxiety, a strange taste or smell, even musical sounds or visual disturbance. Auras are not necessarily followed by a tonic clonic seizure. Where this does happen, it is known as a secondary generalised seizure. Some people report a sense of heaviness, depression or general feeling of not being quite right in themselves before a seizure. This experience can happen for hours or days before they have a seizure. Doctors call this a prodrome, and if a person can learn to recognise this, it can be a useful guide. When a person has no warning, this obviously has its drawbacks as the person does not have a chance to ensure their safety beforehand. Unfortunately, it is this lack of warning that can result in accidents or injury. People who have this type of seizure need to be a little more safety conscious than others paramedics really are the most important people possible we must realise this have been in so many.

So were these the problem?

Sudden Shock!

Well on Monday 14th September 1987, while in Staff ord. I started to study my BTEC Diploma in Business and Finance at the Main Tenderbanks Building of Stafford College. This would start off superb because I went on to pass my First Diploma. In Business and Finance this at this College. At around the same time of 1988 I also went directly into a for training where I started doing some training work in Stafford then Boston hospital whilst studding in Harvard University. On the school report I was to have very good results. It says: My efforts, ability, Assignment work quality, Assignment work return, Overall Skills Grade, Attendance and Punctuality, were all above average. Whilst also results in Working Organisations, Finance, Information Processing, Sales, Keyboarding and Production. My ability with all was also quite good along in Assignment work and Quality, Assignment Return and Overall Skills. The acceptance and passing of my work was fantastic news. Soon on I went and after passing my first diploma. Next it was time to start my second diploma in Business and Finance again at Harvard University. But something shocking was to happen while in a lesson at the school.

Unexpectedly I collapsed then my body unfortunately started going into muscle spasms. Suddenly I was jerking, twitching, and everything all over the floor. Immediately an ambulance came and took me onto Pilgrim hospital on Sibsey Road Boston Lincolnshire in Boston of America Hospital Boston

Luckily Pilgrim hospital then called my mother to tell her what had happened. Then a few days later it was off again for more tests now at the Aston University so now studying time at Queen Elizabeth plus Pilgrim hospitals. But what I was hoping not to be told was confirmed. "We are sorry to tell you Lee, you're now having Partial epileptic seizures in the daytime!" now that was drastic news. I was now also having daytime epileptic seizures!

Then more bad news, "Lee, due to the severity of these seizures you now suffer, we will have to take you off your BTEC second diploma here at Harvard University." This now crushing and ruining my chance of the diploma and many options for future work. Now looking at this it really makes me wonder as to why understanding and knowledge of epilepsy is so bad!" So, on I went now surrounded with all of this shocking news of losing my health and losing my chance of university.

What should I do?

Whilst observing anybody collapsing onto the floor and seeing them go into an epileptic seizure. Please could you firstly try to helping them not to collapse onto the floor if unable put something soft underneath their head whilst making sure the body is stable and not in danger of colliding into anything around them eventually myself included help the body relax but do not hold any part of them just make sure injuries as mentioned to their body are not possible eventually the seizure will slow down and stop once coming around the person should be fully conscious and sometimes somewhat confused for a minute but after one or two everything should be back to normal.

John Kennedy

General Public

This is something people need to do for a person when a person is having an Epileptic seizure. I would and still cannot believe the ignorance about the condition. If my friends from hospitals had not discussed the severity and misfortune of epilepsy like myself. And not explained all about the condition to medical services and the general public. Then maybe they would have not sat down, listened and started to understand as they are now around the world. Because anybody at anytime could wake up. With a health problem of which I have unfortunately experienced.

The medical education and Health Services will always be needed.

What many people have to do is set aside the arrogant kind of person while getting on with general things in life. But still not forgetting there are many other people around the world suffering in some way as well as themselves. Because somebody who has been misplaced with a disability. Then put into an unpredicted position like myself. Should always think I can do that job and accomplish my ambition. Then you will achieve all of your dreams in life. Proving citizens with a disability are just as capable as any other citizenry of performing and completing activities. Epilepsy can be divided into simple partial and complex partial seizures. In a simple partial seizure you are fully conscious. You remain fully aware of your surroundings. However this does not mean that you are able to stop or control the symptoms. In a complex partial seizure you partly lose consciousness and you are not aware of what you are doing.

Because of this, you may not remember the seizure afterwards, or your memory of it will be unclear. The symptoms that you experience depend on which area of your brain is affected by epileptic activity. After being studied I was having partial seizures which involved epileptic activity in just a part of the brain. The disbelief to me is unexplainable. So what were these tingling, giggling sensations? They were now to be studied a lot more deeply and I was told they could be a form of Epileptic Aura. So this dreadfully could have been the problem that had been driving me confused for years!!!

Fun and Employment

Well now it was time to get on with life through confidence and determniation. So on most Mondays such as 22nd June 1987, I would be going down to play squash this is at the local sports centre named Riverside in Stafford plus reaching many meetings around for health care involving many countries around the world

You have the health service in America Medicaid and Medicaid whilst in Britain the is the National Health Service reaching for support you can find so many belonging to countries.

Let me explain the first American policy Medicaid provides health coverage to millions of Americans, including eligible low-income adults, children, pregnant women, elderly adults and people with disabilities. Medicaid is administered by states, according to federal requirements. The program is funded jointly by states and the federal government.

Along with this you also as mentioned earlier Medicare this is the federal health insurance program for people who are 65 or older, certain younger people with disabilities, and people with End-Stage Renal Disease (permanent kidney failure requiring dialysis or a transplant, sometimes called ESRD).

Along the line in Britain the bill called the National Health Service follows everything and is for free It was born out of a long-held ideal that good healthcare should be available to all, regardless of wealth – one of the NHS's core principles. With the exception of some charges, such as prescriptions, optical services and dental services, the NHS in England remains free at the point of use for all UK residents.

Another subject around me was in 1989, I found employment with a lot of help from mum's husband. My very good friend Howard. The job was found in Walsall and Manhattan. They were an Industrial Company named Stephen Glovers where I would work for ten years whilst at the same time medical talks around different countries and hospitals such as the New York Downtown Hospital of the major one following epilepsy and that was in and still is being the Mayo Clinic at Phoenix of Arizona.

Constantly I was now either doing medical talks or helping people looing into Neurology and Psychology whilst employed checking Iron castings click-clicking them together checking for any cracks. Often also using a gauge to inspect and make sure that the Iron castings had been drilled into accurately. I would then count and pack the castings into boxes. This until the table was empty then refilling the table again with very heavy trays of these iron tubing castings.

-Next I would label the different types of boxes and put them up onto shelves. Or take them over to people who were packing the objects. Into other larger boxes and put them onto the trucks outside of the factory and into Lorries. It certainly kept me in good shape for future sports to come.

Unfortunately though day after day at rhythmic peak times. I would often be regularly picking myself up off the floor. This still after having had numerous amounts of grand mal seizures. Funny though because around all of the problems of this neurological health condition. While working on Monday to Friday's from 9.00am—5.00pm throughout the week. My manager Brian would constantly still be telling me off for messing around at work just like I did at school.

Now then around all of this I still had many good times seeing family over in Stafford or Vanvouver of Canada seeing the Canadian Soccer different to the European shall explained to you later.

Whether in the factory or outside of work in Manhattan at my new home town of New York in 1989 well along with my dad Howard as mentioned we both started up a one 5-a side soccer side and decided to name the team Stafford Albion. This was set up to also be playing with my best mate Robert Murphy who I had met at the Stafford Youth Training Scheme. We had both named the team Stafford Albion. Due to us living in Stafford and Albion because of me supporting West Bromwich Albion.

Well after Murph, as I called Rob and some of his mates met up. Every Friday night along with Howard we would all go off into numerous US States could be Dallas or Boston seeing the Red socks so many 50 in all with fifty US Senators keeping the country together playing soccer. At the same time by now we had also started training on Sunday mornings. This at Riverside leisure centre, the building I have mentioned earlier where I was playing Squash in leagued. Well while playing soccer in Birmingham of Alabama and eventually Manchester in Connecticut. The team did very well playing together for four years, winning two league and cup trophies. Also in 1989, after socialising I started helping different social service support groups. This was to be at North Walls in Stafford. The first group

70

I connected with was to help people with Epilepsy. This group was named The New York Epilepsy Support Group why is there no policy from the Government where I met up with a mate. Well we got the group rolling by word of mouth then making it much larger. Often people in the group would meet up. Maybe arrange to do things like go out bowling or maybe browse around the pubs. Just joining up to forget about the epilepsy and defiantly having a good laugh.

After all of the holidays since my childhood now I had started to visit other places around Europe. Now I had started going around the entire world.

No Damage

Something funny well now then on one of my visits to Portugal. I had two totally unexpected experiences. While attempting to play golf with my dad and Granddad Geoff I went to hit a golf ball across the golf pitch. Oh, well what did I do? I had hit the ball across the other side of the golf course. But not only was it the other side of this golf park. It had gone over the grass onto the other pitch by the river.

So I went to get this golf ball and after seeing a tree trunk I decided to cross from one side of the river to the other park. Well, on I went attempting to go across the river and get my ball. Suddenly just half way across Woosh!! I slipped off head first going straight into this river. Funny because I got back out of the river to see my Grandad Geoff who must have been the most unemotional person I have ever met on the floor in stitches laughing next to the putting hole. But the other experience was not quite so funny. Because I was looking over cliff s in part of the Portuguese mountains. When suddenly: I heard "Lee, get back here!" The next thing I picture in my head. Is somebody cutting open my Bryan Ferry tea shirt, "Stop cutting my shirt," I said.

Well what had happened? Unexpectedly I had been knocked out from a sudden fall over the cliff only to come around in this Portuguese hospital. Luckily I would eventually come out a few hours later with only a cut eye brow (leaving a scar over my left eye brow, and at the time a black and swollen eye.) Otherwise I came back to Britain with no damage. Even though I had fallen down this cliff around forty feet only for a bush to save me going down a few thousand feet to death after having an epileptic seizure something else happened in Portugal and that was from sunburn. Since a child I have never had a clue about sun bathing. Well on this one occasion I fell asleep in the sun and woke up the next day red all over with sun burn. Next along with these European trips like Portugal my dad Christopher took my Grandad Geoff and me somewhere for a very special surprise.

World Cup 1990

Well at the beginning of 1990, all was told to me, "Now lee, your Grandad and I are both taking you out to the World Cup this year in Italy." said my dad. I was in quite a bit of shock but also very excited. Well we went out to Italy in the middle of 1990 and watched some massive games, "It is amazing!" I said. We flew out in June of 1990. Dad, Grandad Geoff and Me into Milan watching everything the match became at the end of the time

West Germany 2 – 1 Holland
24th June 1990
Spectators: 74,559
Goals: Kinsmann (60), Brehme (85) for West Germany;
R. Koeman (88, by penalty) for Holland.

First stop was the superb San Siro stadium of Milan with Ruud Gullit, the star of A.C. Milan. On this afternoon, however, Gullit did not find his usual public. He thought he was somewhere else. In the stands, 40,000 German supporters. Opposite, half as many Dutch fanatics. As if the match had been played before the game even started.

From intense, the match was to turn, with the space of one minute, to madness, with the double sending off of Rijkaard and Vollar. Ten men each, and soon one, then two—zero in favour of the pitiless, irresistible West Germany, in the magnificent form of their centre forward Klinsmann. "Germany is going to cure us of all our problems", Rudd Gullit had predicted. Wrong. The Dutchmen had more accurate, more incisive, more dominating merely to reach the level of German players who were becoming stronger and more invincible. West Germany was indeed the monster announced by their coach. Beckenbauer. But who can beat that team? Who can thwart Lothar Mattaus, who rules his team with an iron hand? Italy? We will see but my first visit Milan to this stadium and watching the game was fantastic.

Republic of Ireland 0—0 Romania after extra-time, shoot-out: 5 to 4
Genoa: 25th June 1990
Spectators: 31, 818

Next it was onto Genoa where I was to see a World Cup soccer game go onto penalties. Ireland, or the chef's surprise? Not as much as that. which would be to forget a bit rapidly that the Irish have been unbeaten for two years . . .

Of course, and this was continually repeated, they played incisive football. Without brilliance. But their principle quality is still the exploiting of all the fault teams assumed to be better. And to have no doubts about anything. I, up against the Rumanians, whose mental approach is not really, the Irish did not achieve an overwhelming game, they did not for all that steal their qualification, their goalkeeper, Patty Bonner, having frustrated the Rumanian strikers, and in particular Hagi, one of the largest men in the World Cup.

Brutish and coarse on the field, the Irish are, on the other hand, no less men of quality who draw their faith from the belief in God which they displayed. Pope Jean-Paul II is the only one to be able to boast of causing these Irishmen of fire to lower their heads . . . . Peace be with them!

Next we carried on along watching two other exciting World Cup matches. The other two games were in Bologna and Naples. On 26th June, in the Italian city of Bologna.

England 1—0 Belgium, after extra time
Bologna:
Spectators: 34, 520

The English suffer from no complex unless it is that of superiority! During this match, they had foreseen everything and booked the flight for Naples where their quarter final was to be held. Everything occurred for them as they had imagined. It was, nevertheless, necessary for them to await this goal from David Platt in the final minute of extra time to send them to Naples, where they were to confront the team from the Cameroons. An incredible outcome for a match which was defiantly the most intense, the fi nest of this World Cup; a match which Belgium dominated most often, especially in the first half, thanks to attractive football on the move. But, in this World Cup, playing well is not enough. This was not Belgium's evening. Between a team which wanted a win and another which was waiting for shots at goal, fate hung on for a free kick taken by Gascoigne towards David Platt for a goal which was beautiful and cruel at the same time. For the Belgians, tears; for the English, every hope, including the craziest . . . Watching the World Cup was strange, it really was.

After the third game I explored the Italian city of Florence for the day. Here there were many churches and cathedrals; I walked in and around many very interesting places to hear of a large history in the city. Plus along with this I also had a picture of my face drawn by an artist.

Then it was onto Naples for the fourth game! My dad, grandfather and I were very excited about the prospect. "England played Cameroon!" This played on 1st July 1990, is probably the game most people will not forget for one of numerous reasons.

Me on 1st July 1990 in Naples.
Cameroon 2—3 England, after extra-time.
Naples: 1st July 1990
Spectators: 55, 205.

After David Platt had opened the score half way through the first half, with a dived header, one could believe that was the end of the Cameroons chances. Virtuosos with the trapped ball and specialists in the fi nest offensive sequences of the World Cup, they toyed with the English who were hardly imaginative. Finally, the "Indomitable Lions" were to find the weakness: a penalty from Kunde and a goal by Ekeke brought them to the gates of happiness: a rainbow rose in the sky which was to often choked with a competition which would not allow for improvisation. But the logic of soccer doesn't exist in Africa. Instead of hanging on to the result and locking the game up, the Cameroon players chose a different approach, entirely elegantly and with style, that of all-out attack. Realists and fortunate, the Englishman took advantage of this. Gary Lineker qualified them with two penalties. Glory to the Cameroon and to their players, romantic heralds of a soccer game to come.

Roger Milla was one of the main stars of Italia 90 and was defiantly Cameroon's super substitute at the age of 38, he was one of the oldest players playing in Italia 90, however his performances were breath-taking.

After the England 3—2 Cameroon game on 1st July 1990, I returned back to the United Kingdom. By now the World Cup had got to the stages of the Semi-Finals.

Where on the 3rd July 1990, Italy would take on Argentina in Naples. Then eventually after Extra-tine the match then went onto penalties Italy 4—3 Argentina.

Next on 4th July, West Germany would take on England in Turin. At the Semi-Final match in Turin well there was all but football. Noise, fury and clumsiness in the kick-off of this semi-final, both groups of supporters doing their utmost to whistle the nations anthem of the opponents. But England finished by losing. A pity for the players who deserved better than this pitiful sequence of kicks at goal . . . Two hours of very fi ne football, played in the best possible spirit, with suspense at the end, and the joy of Franz Beckenbauer whom one had never seen so happy, so expansive. After Brehme's goal, the Germans thought they had performed the most difficult bit. But the arrogance of Matthaus colleagues did not shut out moments of doubt. And this doubt grew when Lineker equalised. Since the start of the World Cup, England had not been living up to their talent. It was this very evening when they made this abundantly clear that chance turned her back on them. Cruel. As for Germany, she had gained the right to contest her third consecutive final. A record, so sad. Seeing the game at home thinking how close England was to the final. Still that's life. I remember all well while I was at mum's house in Stafford and watching this match between West Germany and England. The match finished West Germany 1-1 England. Then it went onto penalties where it ended West Germany 4-3 England. But just like as I was as little boy and Dr Who came on. I did the same watching Germany taking penalties against

England and could not bear to watch them as they were taken then hiding behind the sofa.

Next on the television at home I watched 43,000 fans at Bari on 7th July, it was the match between Italy and England. This to see which country would be coming third and fourth in the World Cup. For this match of farewell to his "World Cup" and to his fans, Vicini decided to reinstate the striker duo, Schillaci and Baggio, who had inflamed Italy against Czechoslovakia.

Even though deprived of Gascoigne, one of the superb finds of this month, England, too, were holding their heads high, having been defeated just once in their last twenty-five matches.

A match of honour, therefore, which, happily, provided a sleek and magnificent image of what football still can be.

A sort of attacking fury grasped the players who presented one of the most accomplished spectacles of this World Cup, marred as it was by too many instructions and defensive tactics.

Baggio proved his talent in opening the score through one of the rare mistakes by Peter Shilton, who was playing his last match for England. Without being discouraged, the Englishmen flung themselves into the attack and equalised through Platt.

And then when extra-time was looming, "Toto" Schillaci found himself offered a gift in the form of a penalty. He slotted it in and in this way became the highest goal scorer of this World Cup with six goals. Bari and all of Italy had consolation, whereas the players left the competition arm in arm. England had been the fair-play team . . . England 1 v 2 Italy.

Next on Sunday 8th July, it was the World Cup final, with 73,500 spectators and all in England watching the soccer in Rome the capital of Italy. What will remain in ten, twenty years from this final, the fourteenth in the history of the World Cup? One line, just one, and that will be quite sufficient: West Germany 1-0 Argentina.

The goal scored by a penalty at six minutes before the end by Andreas Brehme, perhaps the most complete player of this World Cup who was so avaricious for goals that he became sad, and who gave rise to so many refereeing incidents that sometimes he was so many referring incidents that sometimes he was ludicrous. The historians will recall that on this Sunday, 8th July 1990, the Germans joined, amongst the medal winners and the competition, Italy and Brazil, who were until now the only two countries to have won the World Cup on three occasions.

Perhaps they will place the accent on Diego Maradona, the almost succeeded in his player of the eighties, who almost succeeded in his dream: to become the first to win the competition twice as captain. At the end of the match, Diego was to break down in tears, like a child deprived of Christmas.

The greatest experts will bring out the fact that with two players sent off – Monzon and Dezotti – Argentina set up a record, which will certainly be diffi cult to beat. As regards the rest, we must forget, and we will all have forgotten very quickly . . .

Maybe next time for England.

CHAPTER THREE

TEMPORAL LOBE

On 27th August 1990, having now reached the age of nineteen my life was to really change. I was still working and studying at Uni speaking regularly to friends of Harvard University up in Boston aiming around everything could reach 10 seizures daily being if where and when with me at the time in work or playing sports on Friday or Saturdays with mates for Stafford Albion. Whist also back at home maybe also reading about the Kennedy's in America. Who by now I seemed to have a big interest in after having been deep into the family history of the Kennedy and now Trump family.

Unbelievably time arrived because in November of 1991, this was when I was to discuss all subjects with Professor Polkey at the Maudsley and soon the Mayo hospital the first in London and the Clinic in Phoenix. Surely I could only expect to be talking to doctors and neurologists about electrode tests at the most! If yes, where will the electrodes be put? On my head, up my shoulders, no not for me I always get the best deal!

Yes, it was electrodes! But electrodes, not on the head!

They were inserted into my skull near my brain! Believe it! You bet! But again that is only the start of the story! As I said: When you feel miserable, think of something that makes you happy! That will cheer you up! Plus do not forget about your hopes and ambitions of tomorrow . . .

So I stayed at the Maudsley Hospital of London in the intensive care department at the time undergoing intracranial because along came the Tests and Procedures EEG (electroencephalogram)

EEG tests for a few days. Unfortunately, I was to stay fully conscious for these tests until I had enough seizures. I would have five seizures in all for Neurologists to identify. Where the troubled abnormal nerve cells were coming from in the brain Well after the tests I then came home and went back to work in sities and states like Boston or Walsall.

Well on into reaching 1992, suddenly excitement why, well because while I was still living in Manhattan or Stafford with my Mum and Howard. Our family had the pleasure of my Aunty Diane's son coming into the world. His name is Thomas Jay Cawley who was born on Saturday 7th March 1991.

Now around all of my health problems that were there. I often still had fun doing and watching interesting things. I started to play an electric keyboard going regularly go for lessons in Stafford town centre while also playing tunes in my bedroom. All around while looking after Tom, while he often stayed with us as a little boy. Also myself I still played soccer with Stafford Albion and watching the Albion in West Bromwich. It was all good fun!

Extraordinarily on Saturday 25th April 1992, while all of this was going on Howard and my Mum. Well they were suddenly to arrange something very special for my twenty first birthday. I was invited to West Bromwich Albion Soccer Club. Where I went and met all of the West Bromwich Albion players I had a fantastic day! The Albion even won:

West Bromwich Albion 3—0 Preston North End.

Around all of this unfortunately everything had again started. Because I was now having conversations with and letters from the Maudsley Hospital in London. This with my neurologists and surgeons after the EEG tests concerning surgery which would be happening sometime in 1992.

All while still, going outside of our house in Stafford. Working in major cities I was enjoying life in around with sports. But it was still test after tests while in hospital having EEG, CAT and MRI Scans. Hospitals could still not detect where these abnormal nerve cells of the brain. Had been coming from and if it was a brain tumour. Well because still since a child, everything had always read normal. So what was causing the problem?

While working full-time I still did college courses in Harvard. On one occasion just as I was about to start a nightly course named the R.S.A. Clait something funny happened. Because as I walked into the class room I saw somebody very special unexpectedly it was my Aunty Diane who would also be doing the R.S.A. course as well. In the course we would be using Microsoft Office programs Word for word processing, Excel for spread sheets and Access for database, which my Aunt and I passed easily.

After this course I went onto a graphics course where something hilarious was to happen. In the class while working on computers the tutor, well she would often leave the room. I assume to other classrooms by the door for a minute. So when doing this often I went onto the Internet. Looking different things up from English soccer to American politics seeing what I could find on the subjects. On the one occasion while the tutor was out of the room. I studied onto the internet and typed in (www.whitehouse.com) now when typing this into the computer I was expecting something concerning American politics and Bill Clinton to appear.

To my shock when I pressed enter a new web page. This expectedly came up with medical health serviceso around me started laughing along with me. But, then the tutor suddenly came back into the class room. To see the pornography web page on the screen, she was not very impressed.

But we explained all and I explained to her for going onto the internet while in the course.

Well, after having received results from the implantation of subdural and depth electrodes. I returned to the Maudsley Hospital at Denmark Hill in London. Next I was discussing all with my surgeon Professor Polkey. I was told there had been detection of damage to my brain. The damage was on the left temporal lobe of my brain:

The temporal lobes, one on each side of the head, just above the ears, are the sites of one of the most common forms of epilepsy. Complex partial seizures with automatisms (unconscious actions), such as lip smacking or rubbing the hands together, are the most common seizures in temporal lobe epilepsy.

Seventy-five per cent of patients also experience simple partial seizures which may include such features as: a mixture of thoughts, emotions, and feelings that are hard to describe; sudden emergence of old memories or feelings of strangeness in familiar surroundings; hallucinations of voices, music, smells, or tastes, and feelings of unusual fear or joy. While partial seizures dominate, approximately half the people with temporal lobe epilepsy have generalized tonic-clonic seizures as well.

The seizures characteristics of temporal lobe epilepsy often begin in the deeper parts of the temporal lobe (part of the limbic system) which control emotions and memory.

Memory problems may develop over time in people with this syndrome.

Twenty-Five Percent Chance

Now the question would be: What should I do and where do I go next? Well it was time to make an undesirable decision.

This following the subdural and depth electrode tests as to whether or not to undergo with the surgery. This operation had a 25 per cent chance of total success. "What are the risks to Left temporal lobe lobotomy, (Brain Surgery)?" I asked Professor Polkey. "This is the left temporal side of the brain!" Professor Polkey replied. "There is a 25 per cent chance of success in curing you, Lee! "There is a 25 per cent chance of your health improving! "While also having a 25 per cent chance of your health staying the same! "Also maybe a 25 per cent chance of the epilepsy maybe deteriorating! "Plus, then there might be troubles of the right side of your body becoming paralysed!" he said. Why paralysed? I asked. "This is because the left side of the brain controls the right of the body." He said.

So on Sunday 20th September 1992, on I went into the Maudsley hospital. We had found out by then that I was to undergo brain surgery on the left temporal resection of my brain to improve my epilepsy. Well on Monday 21st September 1992 it was time for the big day. From what I remember on that night before the operation was while I was in bed.

A Doctor came into the room "Lee, we just need to let you have a little sleep for tonight and we will wake you in the morning." "O.K." I said. The next thing I remember is waking up the next day of 23rd October 1992.

Unbeknown to me I had obviously undergone the surgery because of what I saw in the mirror.

Well I looked at my face in the mirror and the left hand side was so swollen it was unreal. Eventually I was starting to feel where the bruising was and suffered a few headaches for nine days. I hoped and prayed this operation had worked and not to have another seizure. But unfortunately it was not to come true. Two days later I had my first seizure again.

Even though this happened there was still some success due to that day in the operation room. Because they had started to find out as to where the problem was that had been causing sudden Grand Mal seizures. Plus also the surgeons had erased the red rash from the left side of my cheek bone.

But still there was no understanding or cure of these horrible tingling sensations in my stomach.

Eventually on Sunday 4th October 1992, I came out of hospital and coming back up to Staff ord. After a few weeks the swelling of my head had gone. After recovery I went back into work at the industrial company in Walsall. But I was still regularly collapsing and ending up in Walsall hospital.

But every time I got up and carried on with determination.

This to beat the neurological problem I had come down with as a teenager called epilepsy.

Are you talking about me?

Well September 1993, began and after the age of 22 the good, bad and the ugly unfortunately started. Suddenly my personality and attitude unexpectedly changed. My patience and tolerance with others became terrible. I was becoming very suspicious of people. Then "Are you talking about me?" I would often abruptly comment also becoming very paranoid. Sometimes at work I would think work mates were dropping boxes on the floor to make noises on purpose to annoy me. I regularly suffered delusions. These would be such things while awake or asleep like hearing noises, stinks and many other things. Th is all due to some stupid reducing of a tablet for epilepsy named Clonazipan.

Now I would be arguing at home as well! Silly things would irritate me, such as smells of food! On one occasion I was upstairs when suddenly I could smell some bacon.

So running down the stairs, "What's that smell! "You're cooking that on purpose, aren't you, Mum!!" I would say.

Another time Mum was cooking me pie and mash. Th en I walked into the kitchen and threw all the food into the bin!

These problems were all causing so much trouble for my family at the time. Now it was time for more work with neurologists and doctors at the Queen Elizabeth hospital of Edgbaston in Birmingham. I would eventually find out my doctors had been reducing the Clonazipan at too much of a fast rate as mentioned. This then suddenly causing side effects called incipient psychosis.

Psychosis is a loss of contact with reality, usually including false ideas about what is taking place or who one is (delusions) and seeing or hearing things that aren't there (hallucinations). So why were people talking about me? I would say to neurologists and psychiatrists.

Well, this reason for me having problems of thinking like this and changing my personality at times was all due to Chemical Imbalances. "Whizzing!" around in my brain.

Still I would be accusing my mum and Howard of saying or doing things. By now constantly shouting due to these thoughts that they were talking about me or saying things to people concerning me. When really they were not talking about me or doing anything at all. It was the suspicion in the mind and now suffering with psychosis. So now it was time gain for even more tablets but these were for a psychological problem not the neurological problem of epilepsy. This new tablet for psychosis imbalances was named Haloperidol.

So throughout all of mid-1993 and early 1994, I was to be going back and forth to hospital in Edgbaston.

This my mom and I did regularly, each month. One of our unfortunate experiences was when going over to the hospital. Suddenly, "Stop going over this ramp on purpose, Mum!!" I shouted.

This because as my mum drove her car to the Queen Elizabeth Hospital in Birmingham. We would be going down a steep road onto the car park. It went bump, bump, bump, over the ramp. Then I got very irritated!!

I had pains and noises that would provoke me. I would feel as though I was going to have a seizure any minute! Maybe bring a painful sensation into my arms! Also noises!

It was both terrible for my family and me, all due to the reducing of a tablet to fast!

Often I have heard so much about people who suffer the problem of psychosis, "He may commit suicide!" say doctors. When suffering with this problem what happens is you start to imagine and suspect! I would often still think about the past cheering me up. But the problem was suspecting people talking, about me and doing things on purpose to annoy me. I never had any ideas of suicide who ever says that makes the whole situation for the parents and patient twice as bad.

After the explaining of psychosis I insert the social care workers letter. Basically what good ideas of successful things are there to then stop some of many different psychological problems? As mentioned, activeness, going out and associating, are all best. Medication can help but does not always work. It is what you psychologically think that matters. It is good to have a chat with family and friends sometimes about your problems. Throughout all of this I was put onto a tablet named Primozide and later Haloperidol as mentioned plus Procylidine to try and get the problems out of my system. Eventually the medication and my genuine personality all started to combine and everything went back to normal.

The guess was all to do with fiddling around with my medication, nothing to do with me.

The neurologists, "Our guess is that this odd psychotic state may relate to the slow withdrawal of Clonazepam." They said. What may have happened is that we have unpeeled the Clonazepam off his Benzodiazepine receptors it has made them more vulnerable to the Vigabitran and its psychosis inducing properties. I therefore think it is right to continue withdrawing Lee from it."

At the time I did not realise what was going on, but now I remember all and think qualify people making such mistakes how terrible! I hope it does not happen again, because that was stupid! I would and still do think about what happened concerning the reducing of that medication.

Do not forget I am a human now treat me like one please. All the way throughout this my mum and family would constantly understand and help me to get through the problem.

In 1992, one dream from childhood came along because West Bromwich Albion got to Wembley in London of the United Kingdom. In 1992–93 Albion finished fourth and entered the playoff s for the fi rst time, having just missed out the previous year. Albion's fi rst appearance at Wembley for over twenty years—and their last ever at the original stadium—saw them beat Port Vale 3–0 to return to the second level – now renamed the First Division.

Later I will talk more about the neurological problems of epilepsy. Whilst also the more enjoyment and fun throughout life. Now in the next chapter many of my dreams and ambitions were to really come true in and around having had the first form of left temporal lobe surgery back in 1992. By now I still dreamed of visiting one country. This was the United States of America, would I ever well studying and hospitals done plus meetings?

CHAPTER FOUR

EXPLORING THE WORLD!!

Party Time

Now I mention about some more vacations around the world.

Of which I had arraigned and have been on by myself. Or at other times which were organised with friends. Well the first vacation I did was on 21ˢᵗ July 1993, with some friends. We started off by leaving Dover of England on past Dunkirk of France and into Switzerland.

Along the way I saw the terrible remains from D-Day of June 6ᵗʰ 1944. The beaches at Dunkirk invaded were Utah Beach, Omaha beach onto Gold Beach. Also on the same day the English and Canadians went into Juno beach and Sword beach.

My Granddad George has told me so much about his times from World War Two. He went on into Juno beach with the Canadians. At the time going over into the beaches from the HMS Salamander ship. Grandad went from Southampton by ship. To eventually go onto one of the five islands as mentioned called Juno Beach at Dunkirk.

On reaching the beach the army then had to go through wire fencing to invade and get past the Germans. This was the start of where many people from Canada and England were to lose their lives. All due to Nazi Germany of World War Two.

Anyway while on my touring of Switzerland with friends in 1993. There was the bus up to Nufenenpass (7600ft) of which I walked around to the reservoir – Griessee. We all then went around to Gries Glacier, back down to the dam and up to Griespass. This was at 2479m – 818 feet of which is the border between Switzerland and Italy.

Mountains in Switzerland 1993

While having a good laugh we all then went into Leukerbad. Next it was onto the town of Lucerne of which we visited the town for a day. At the same time we were to visit and then go on to stay in Obergsten.

On the 1st August 2003, we all went onto a Swiss National Day in Interlaken. Swiss National Day is the time for cultivating numerous national customs and traditions.

Festive highlights include bonfires lit high up on the mountain slopes, well visible from below. This is a feast of folklore with alphorn blowing, flag throwing and yodelling.

Children especially love the evening lantern procession and grand fi rework display. Many villages and alps also organize a special brunch to celebrate Switzerland's birthday.

I had a lot of fun as we all watched the people. Who were all dressed up in different costumes for the show. These such as a hulk, another was one lady wearing a Swiss football strip. Also people were playing Karate as they all went along streets. Others on the show were many people going around on old trucks and carts. Where some horses would be moving along the motors. It was so much fun to see. Eventually we stayed back in Obergsten for the night. But on 5th August 1993, came back into Dover of the United Kingdom. Then on arriving back home to Staff ord. It was again time for work down in Walsall of the West Midlands.

Great Thanks!!

Expectations came in late 1993, I was to finally experience something. This had been one of my immense dreams since childhood living in America!

Nseow my thoughts had finally come back into perspective after having recovered from psychosis six months earlier in Staff ord. All due to the immense speed in reducing of my medication by neurologists from the Queen Elizabeth Hospital in Birmingham of the West Midlands in England.

Now I would and still do think, as long as you bring a nice personality into the world. Your dreams in life will always come true. So now I started to think. At the age of twenty-three, how do I get around to staying in America personally? This whilst also working full time.

Well in mid-1993, suddenly out of the blue something happened. This just after contacting the British politicians Support Group in Leeds where the supporters of while Tony Blair very kindly gave me a telephone number. The phone number was for the main American Capital Hill Senate. This of which is based just off Pennsylvania like the White House in the American state as just mentioned just sentaring America's capital Washington D.C. So, I passed the telephone number on to my mum. Then she made a telephone call to them for me from her work Unexpectedly a week later I received a letter from America. This offering me to make my first visit to the United States of America. It was unbelievable! The lady whom my mum had spoken to at the support group invited me to America, Never! I thought. Also requesting me to put down in writing to the support group as to places I would like to visit in the United States of America.

Heath Care & Reform.

Amazingly my dream finally became true on 21st of July 1994. America!! Well I started by flying into Connecticut. Then aiming to fly into Baltimore-Washington airport. Funny because on arriving into the airport I started to notice and very much so whilst staying in America and that reaches over about public personality comes over much broader abnd social to the British. Looking everywhere strangely nobody understood as to the liking of my accent? In America you have plenty of social invitations.

Well the flight finally arrived into Maryland. My expanded knowledge finally had been prevised I was in America. Now I was here to have a fantastic time. While touring Baltimore I saw many amazing places whist soon to be also experiencing one of the most amazing days of my life.

On the first few days I visited new places such as Baltimore's National Aquarium. Where I saw a great show with the many different fish, birds, and dolphins.

Well on my new visit into Washington D.C. I was taken around onto a tour of the F.B.I. building. Or the J.Edgar Hoover, Federal borough Investigation building in Washington D.C. Around the building, I saw such things as the Lee Harvey Oswald shot gun. This was the gun that supposedly killed President Kennedy.

Whilst also in the Federal Borough Investigation building. We saw a show by an F.B.I agent. Where they were to do a show by shooting against a wooden board that looked like a body. She took shots at the board with a thirty-eight revolver. Where at an unbelievable speed she made a circle around the wooden board's head. It was amazing especially at the speed and direction of the shots taken. After being in Baltimore for four days, the lady named Sandra who had invited me over came back home. At that time from her work out in Baltimore with two surprises for me. One of the surprises was that in the next couple of days.

I would be seeing Washington's Capitol Hill, home of all working senators. The other she told me was quite a massive surprise. Of which was to be on the next day, it was quite a shock to me.

So I visited Washington D.C. on the 26th of July 1994, along with my friends of the American foundation of Maryland. Where we went into one of the rooms and onto a meeting.

Although the United States has never had a universal health care system, it does have certain publicly funded health care programs that help to provide for the elderly and disabled (via Medicare), military service families, veterans (via the Veterans Health Administration), and some of the poor (via Medicaid), and children via S-CHIP. Additionally, federal law guarantees public access to emergency services regardless of ability to pay. Bill Clinton had campaigned heavily on health care in the 1992 election. Well this meeting was about that subject of health

Care in the United States of America. Suddenly then while waiting for the meeting to start, out came Senator Edward Moore Kennedy. I could not believe it!! After doing his speech he then came over to people in the crowd. Suddenly, I had the honour of meeting him when he came over to myself and others at the meeting. At that moment of shaking my hand luckily I also had a postcard. The post card had the three Kennedy's on John, Bobby and Ted Kennedy. "Mr Kennedy could you sign this for me please?" I asked. "Yes, certainly." He replied. "I have a very big interest in your family." I mentioned, "Thank you!" He said. Then we both shook hands and Senator Edward Moore Kennedy left the room. I was in shock I had met a Kennedy. The picture with his signed autograph now stands high on my bedroom wall. I wondered as to how and what Senator

Edward Moore Kennedy would write as a signature. Well always signed something with his name as Ted Kennedy.

Caption: Senator Ted Kennedy above.

Th e Big Apple and IMAX

After meeting Kennedy it was time to add more to my fantastic tour. Such as Washington D.C.'s Capitol Hill. Th is being where all American Senators such as Kennedy often work. Then it was onto the Pentagon and also the National Air and Space Museum both also in Washington. D.C.

TED and ROSE KENNEDY BRAIN SURGERY

Well on the 29th June 1994, it was time to see New York. So my friend Andy drove into New Jersey. It had taken us four hours to reach from Baltimore. Th en Nicole, Ryan and I got a train from New Jersey's Metro station and into New York's Penn Station. Of which took us around half an hour. On our first day we took a minibuses tour of Manhattan's buildings the areas buildings were so large.

On the next day while visiting Manhattan we all managed to see the World Trade Center it was massive. We went into the south tower. Where the elevator went from the ground and up to the hundred and seventh floor in less than sixty seconds.

On reaching the 107th floor you could see all of Manhattan. This was through the windows of the World Trade Center Restaurant (the world's highest) occupied. We all went to the top observation deck, in the South Tower of The twin towers; with 110 floors rising 1,353 feet the view of Manhattan was amazing, it was possible to see 45 miles in every direction.

After returning to Baltimore I was then off to Orlando in Florida.

I flew out on 1st August 1994 memories still come back also of 09 September 2001 when some saw everything from screen whilst my personal memories come back in being at the night of when the Trade Centre being there was terrible as it became hit by two planes. The centre blew up and everything reached over horrific as mentioned 107 floor building in two were blowned up people were running everywhere

When arriving into the city, a local named mate Chuck from the local Association of Central Florida, was there with a young girl named Jemma both there to pick me up. On the two days of staying in Florida, a lovely lady named Dott and her husband Jeff were they're inviting me to stay with them in Orlando. There I met up with people from the Epilepsy Support Group. The next day I was invited to see the Kennedy Space Center in Orlando. At the Space Center we saw an IMAX version screen. Th is would explain about the Space Center and the Shuttle's that go around the Space Center, located on Cape Canaveral. Of which offers you a guided bus tour, there you can see the actual launch sites. Plus an exciting hands-on spacecraft exhibit. We also viewed "The Dream is Alive", on this IMAX (5-story screen) movie filmed partly from the space shuttle itself. Astronauts say it is the next-best thing to actually being in space!

Eventually after the two days in Orlando I flew back into Baltimore-Washington airport. This after having had a great visit into Florida. For the next couple of days a friend of Nicole's named Kel was to take me around many places. On my trip he also took me around my favourite city Washington D.C. where we also saw the White House.

On getting to the building we tried to get onto the White House tour. Th is by saying we had lost our tickets but it did not work.

I think the funniest of all that Kel and I managed was when making a visit to the cinema at the start of my American trip. When arriving in I asked for some popcorn, the thing was though people serving said "Would you like cheese on it" "Yak" I thought popcorn was always sweet with sugar, but in the USA I certainly learnt it is also made with salt.

Suddenly on 4th August 1994, flying back to Britain just as we were to take off from Cincinnati. Unexpectedly there was a flight delay because gasoline needed to be reloaded in to the plane. Funny because I found out on getting back to the leaving room for my fl ight from Cincinnati back to Gatwick was that the plane full of people had been waiting for me. What an honour!

But just as we were landing back into Gatwick Airport suddenly something shocking happened because the left wing of the plane set on fi re. Thankfully we all landed and came out of the plane safe. But unexpectedly my luggage was still at Cincinnati in America. Eventually I picked my suitcase up a couple of days later along with my second piece of luggage. Th is of which was a golf club I had brought back from the USA for Howard. Well the airport thought it was a shotgun. But eventually then returned it to me, great fi rst visit with many more to come.

Whoosh

Around the work and support year of returning throughtout eventually one of many more visiting was made into America well the Friday 21st July 1995, I made my next visit to Oakland which is the eighth-largest city in the U.S. state of California. Also it is a major West Coast port, located on San Francisco plenty to see and do having been nito so many visits surrounding America and obviously Harvard Univercity with the Boston Redocks that though is in Massacusis. San Fransisco has so much to give colour is the number one

The Bay, about 8 miles (13 km) east of San Francisco. San Francisco is famous for its hills. Th ere are more than 50 hills within city limits. Some neighbourhoods are named after the hill on which they are situated, including Nob Hill, Pacific Heights, and Russian Hill. Near the geographic center of the city, southwest of the downtown area, are a series of less densely populated hills. Twin Peaks, a pair of hills resting at one of the city's highest points, forms a popular overlook spot. San Francisco's tallest hill, Mount Davidson, is 925 feet (282 m) high and is capped with a 103 foot (31 m) tall cross built in 1934. Dominating this area is Sutro Tower, a large red and white radio and television transmission tower. While staying in Oakland I personally saw some amazing sites and seen's whilst making some very interesting tours such as views of the San Francisco Bay. There was the ferry ride I did out to the island of Alcatraz. This is where all of the tourists were wearing ear plugs for this audio tour of the building. It is a world unto itself. Isolation, one of the constants of island life for any inhabitant—soldier, guard, prisoner, Indian, bird or plant is a recurrent theme in the unfolding history of Alcatraz. This is an old Prison from many years ago. Now on this vacation to California I also visited Sausalito and Berkley.

But suddenly when back into San Francisco. I did another tour taking some very interesting photographs. Well this tour was a helicopter tour it was great being my first and favourite. But quite a bright helicopter tour at the same time over San Francisco.

Golden Gate Bridge from helicopter in 1995.

Suddenly while doing the tour over many beautiful mountains of San Francisco. We went all over and around the Oakland Bay Bridge and San Francisco bay mountains.

Well unexpectedly as we were flying through the air. The helicopter polite: "Would you like to go under the Golden Gate Bridge in the helicopter?" he said. Well I thought he was joking but as we came to the bridge. But suddenly Whoosh!!! Straight under the Golden Gate Bridge we went in the helicopter, oh did I jump in horror.

The Golden Gate Bridge is a suspension bridge spanning the Golden Gate, the opening of the San Francisco Bay into the Pacific Ocean. As part of both U.S. Route 101 and California State Route 1, it connects the city of San Francisco on the northern tip of the San Francisco Peninsula to Marin County. Th e weight of the roadway is hung from two cables that pass through the two main towers and are fi xed in concrete at each end. Each cable is made of 27,572 strands of wire. Th ere are 80,000 miles (129,000 km) of wire in the main cables. Th e bridge has approximately 1,200,000 total rivets. So you can understand what I mean! Somehow though on developing the photographs I took with my camera there were some quite good shots of the city.

Th en and after having been in California for two weeks I returned to England on Th ursday 3rd August 1995.

Address a home ideas for New York

CHAPTER FIVE

NEW PROPERTY AND FUN!!

Back in England and Manhattan November 1996, my health and life seemed to be very good. Suddenly though around all of the working at the Medical talking in the states it was time for me to move on and have my own property.

So on 26th November 1996, in Manhattan. I bought a nice one bed roomed fl at costing me £32,000. I put down £7,000, then coming on to have a mortgage of £25,000. A very exciting time! While every day I still working at so much and supporting the Baggies in West Bromwich or New York of the city of Manhattan. While living there I had a lot of fun with my mates. Th ere were many interesting things to enjoy. Quite funny because not only would I go down to the gym but my cooking was fantastic as well. Every morning it would be porridge, in the afternoon it would be a sandwich of some form. Th en at night it was my own personal recipe. What was that? Well it was pasta! I had not got a clue how to cook. Th e amount of times I sent the fi re alarm off was unbelievable. At times I would be trying to cook bacon under the grill. Th en I would go off and do something else. But suddenly: "Oh no!" I would say to myself. I could smell smoke and this would be the bacon or sausages. Cooking under the grill and on fi re! So I would either put a wet towel over the top. Of the grill or as stupid as it sounds. I would open the kitchen window and throw the grill out. Th is onto the garden outside by cars.

Praying, I had not set on anywhere on fi re and thank god thins did not ever happen!

Next, I have been brought up to be a very clean and tidy person. All of my clothes and items have always been put in cupboards or the fridge ha, ha. Th en another thing I had not got a clue what to do and that was the washing. I was alright at the plates and all in the sink. But ask me how to use a washing machine or how to do the ironing and I was and now am perfect. One time I tried to iron a shirt and burnt a hole into the shirt so that was the end of that long time ago now have learnt how to do loads more.

Luckily my mum lives just around the corner of me in Staff ord. So she would come pick all of my washing up. Th en take it back to her and Howard's house to wash and iron. Next day all clothes and things would be brought back and I would put them away into my cupboards. Around all of this, I would still be going out to work in Walsall or Manhattan and even better going down the gym to learn another form of exercise. Th is was learning how to do aerobics. Aerobics is a form of physical exercise that combines rhythmic aerobic exercise with stretching and strength training routines with the goal of improving all elements of fi tness (fl exibility, muscular strength, and cardio-vascular fi tness)

I remember in my fi rst lesson of aerobics "You are very good at this Lee." girls in the class said. But then in the second lesson what happened? Well of cause, I was trying to be the pretty boy thinking as if I knew everything. But due to me not concentrating, I went and fell over in the class and nearly sprained my ankle. Seeing around twenty ladies laughing at you is not as funny as it sounds. But since then my tutor from that time Dianne has now become a good friend of mine.

Th en of course every Saturday, I would still be at the Albion with my Granddad Geoff. But due to me not beingable to drive, Howard or my mum would very kindly give me a lift to the Albion. Along with another friend of mine Rupert Carthy who also supported West Bromwich Albion.

Later after the soccer I would be out with my mates. Well apart from us joking around as usual with the women. I became very excited if the song "Sweet Child of Mine!" came on because then it was certainly my night. Suddenly my mate Dave and I would be on the stage dancing and going crazy. Me taking "Slash!" the guitarist off from the Los Angeles group Guns and Roses.

Around all of this it would also be hilarious, because my mates, Dave, Eric, John and me. Well we would walk into a night club named the Grapes. Suddenly: "Here he is Ricky Martin the second!!" the D.J. would say. Who was that? Well of cause since my visit to Dallas in 1999 it would be me taking Ricky Martin off every Saturday. So we would get the drinks in and soon it was time for the music. Th en bang up I went and was on the stage by myself taking off the Mexican Ricky Martin. Who is also the same age as me being born in 1971. I would be singing Livin' la Vida Loca!" or other hit songs like "She Bangs!" by Ricky Martin.

Rainbow

More States along the line whilst working or enjoying time in out and surrounding the States property in America and England this became a little story through visiting different places in and revolving different places surrounding in and outside of the world on this occasion it became different states of the US

At Disney we all went around on the tours. But the funniest of all was to happen with Winnie the Pooh. Th ere were many people waiting to have a photograph with him. But of course, when it was my turn to have a photograph with him what happened? Well he walked off and went to the office.

Next Day we visited Universal Studios. Where I went on many rides such as the Jurassic Park Ride, seeing jaws who suddenly came out of the river. Next on the same tour a car came down, I thought it was not going to stop. But luckily it fell just next to everybody on the ride. Eventually I got off very wet and in shock. Th en we visited Death Valley, where I had a photograph taken. Th e thing was though that I had not realised the heat of the area until suddenly going to sit on this wall for the photograph. And "Oh was the wall hot!" I shouted. I thought my backside was on fi re. After all of these tours in Los Angeles it was time to move on to our next state.

Well on the 9th September 96, we arrived into the Grand Canyon where I had a fantastic view of the superb mountains. On the tour over the Grand Canyon I did a helicopter tour taking some nice pictures of the mountains. Some were of the massive Colorado River which runs straight in between the Grand Canyon Mountains.

Afterwards I went to the top of the Grand Canyon Mountains and suddenly just like weather in the United Kingdom it started to poor down with rain. But amazingly out of the blue the rain stopped and a beautiful rainbow appeared out into the sky. Photograph of Rainbow at Grand Canyon. Next we went onto Las Vegas in Nevada on the Th ursday 12h September 1996. Before reaching the city we had to go through the forests. But when arriving into Los Vegas you see so many amazing shows, I started by going into the massive Ceasers Palace. Where I saw so many casino's where the lights from around the building were brilliant. Th en as I went back out of Ceasers Palace and down the long Vegas road I then went onto see Treasure Island. Suddenly the Treasure Island resort opened with the free Buccaneer Bay which has a show in a large man-made lake fronting the resort along the Las Vegas Strip. Presented several times nightly with a large cast of stunt performers, the show depicted the landing and subsequent sacking of a Caribbean village by pirates. Two days later, we went past the Hoover Dam. Th ere are two lanes for automobile traffi c across the top of the dam, which formerly served as the Colorado River crossing. Next it was onto Yosemite National Park, Yosemite is one of the largest and least fragmented habitat blocks in the Sierra Nevada, and the park supports a diversity of plants and animals. Th e park has an elevation range from 2,127 to 13,114 feet (648 to 3,997 m) and contains fi ve major vegetation zones: chaparral/oak woodland, lower montane, upper montane, subalpine, and alpine. Of California's 7,000 plant species, about 50% occur in the Sierra Nevada and more than 20% within Yosemite. Th ere is suitable habitat or documentation for more than 160 rare plants in the park, with rare local geologic formations and unique soils characterizing the restricted ranges many of these plants occupy. Th en we all went back into California and toured San Francisco. Th is time I did not go under the bridge like the helicopter tour. On this occasion I walked across the bridge, feeling a lot safer. After the two days we spent in San Francisco. We all fl ew back into England having had a great two weeks together in America.

Ticket Office

Eventually in April 1999, I was to shoot back out to America again. I started on 23rd April 1999, by visiting friends Dave and Jenni in Gaithersburg of Maryland. Well while staying with them I also visited Washington D.C. and the states Virginia and West Virginia around the area of Maryland. Whilst visiting diff erent parts of America. I went onto a meeting with the American Epilepsy Foundation. Th e discussion was about emplacing of a Vagus Nerve machine.

Th e Vagus nerve stimulation (VNS) is a treatment for epilepsy where a small generator is implanted under the skin below the left collar bone. Th is is connected to a lead with three coils at one end. Th ese coils are wrapped around the vagus nerve in the left side of the neck in a small operation.

Th e VNS stimulates the vagus nerve at intervals to reduce the frequency and intensity of seizures. Suddenly though while out in America on the morning of 27th April 1999, something very interesting happened. I went onto a train from Gaithersburg of Maryland. Th is very early of the morning on 27th April 1999 into a station named the Reagan train station. Th e Reagan train station arrived just outside the Washington Mail of Washington D.C where the station is only two minutes away from the White house and Capitol Hill. Now the Washington Mail is where you stand to get a ticket to tour the White House. Well I was hoping to get a ticket to visit the White House for my twenty-eighth birthday. But on arriving I could not believe it, there were thousands of people cueing and waiting to get one of these tickets. So I waited in the cue until around midday for a ticket to see the White House.

But suddenly "Th ere is no point in waiting any longer you might as well go home." A steward came over and said. So, after hearing this, I then went over to the souvenir shop also by the Washington Mail.

Well while going into the shop I had a look around to see if there was anything to take back with me to England. At the same time thinking to myself hopefully I will be coming back to Washington D.C. again next year. But now a bit upset and refl ecting on things. One being that it is my birthday today and I have not got a ticket to explore the White House. Anyway I picked up a computer disc and calendar then passed all over to a lady for me to pay. Suddenly the person took my items from me and walked off into another room. I wondered where she had gone, as did her workmate. "Do you know where Abbi has gone?" her workmate asked me. "I do not know, also she has walked off with my CD and calendar!" I said.

Well unexpectedly the lady named Abbi, had left the room to go into the back of the shop. But suddenly walking back into the shop store room "You seem like a really nice gentleman, where you from?" she asked. "I am from England." I mentioned. Th en "Where about?" she seemed interested. "I am from Birmingham." I said. Th en "Are you travelling alone." Abbi asked. Yeah, I am travelling alone." I again mentioned. Suddenly "Here is a ticket for the White House." She came out with and said. Well, I was amazed and for once I was lost for words to say. Now for me to have nothing to say to somebody that is quite amazing! After me thanking Abbi off I went to explore the White House on a tour.

Ring, Ring, Ring!!!

Th e White House tour was to be very exciting, oh yes! But also something else was to happen. Just as all the tourists were being checked out by the security guards for weapons in our clothes and bags "Ring, Ring, Ring, Ring, Ring." I went into the White House and the alarms went off. Just like an airport and unbelievably who had set the alarms off all over the White House, typical it was me. What had I done? I had walked into the White House with boots on. Th e metal on my boots had set the alarms off. Th is to the electric gates people have to walk through. I suddenly found out that prohibited items include, but are not limited to, the following: handbags, book bags, backpacks, purses, food and beverages of any kind, strollers, cameras, video recorders or any type of recording device, tobacco products, personal grooming items (make-up, hair brush or comb, lip or hand lotions, etc.), any pointed objects (pens, knitting needles, etc.), aerosol containers, guns, ammunition, fi reworks, electric stun guns, mace, martial arts weapons/devices, or knives of any size. Th e U.S. Secret Service reserves the right to prohibit any other personal items. Umbrellas, wallets, cell phones and car keys are permitted. Well I was then checked out for weapons but eventually allowed to do my tour of the building.

Picture of me outside White House on 27ᵗʰ April 1999.

Now excited I had a good look while being toured around the White House. Th ere were many pictures on the White House walls. One picture of George Washington, another was a drawing of John F Kennedy on the wall just as you walk along the hall. Th ese pictures were on the wall over by the stairs going upstairs to the next fl oor. Th is was all a great experience helped by Abbi from the souvenir shop for my twenty-eight birthday.

Kisses for Ricky!!!

Well on 31ˢᵗ April 1999, after doing a little more touring around Maryland. I shot off fl ying down to Dallas for my next story of America. Well after jetting into Dallas Fort Worth International Airport I got a taxi to the hotel. It was not quite what Lee or Ricky were to be expecting. Eventually the taxi reached my hotel and I walked into the reception putting my suitcase down. Well while having a conversation with the hotel receptionist about my hotel ticket and card to open the door to my room. Suddenly while talking to the lady. I thought she is rather well built for a female with big shoulders and a wide cheek boned face. Also, with a very deep voice, so on and so on thinking that I am sure I have seen her on the Jerry Springer show! I got my card and went up to my room to get changed. After that and still feeling rather jet lagged I went and got a coff ee back down stairs. Th is is the next part and where I started to worry! I turned around suddenly to look over at this very well built lady. She winked. I thought, Oh No! Th en to my shock there mouth opened and this person's tongue came out towards me. As though, come over to me darling, I want to do something! I knew that was a man or transvestite, no thank you! I thought. If you want it choose somebody else by all means sir but you are not having me mate! I also found out they were not only the receptionist but they also owned the hotel. Well after drinking the coff ee fast, I thought, ah Lee let's get out of here and have some fun! So off I went looking around for good pubs and nightclubs. While walking around I saw a pub and it was a karaoke night club pub. Good for a sing, song. So in I went thinking this looks very interesting plenty of people and yes! Lots of women! I walked around and spoke to three good-looking girls Texan women. We started talking most of the night. Th en the singing started and suddenly "Lee, would you sing a song for us please!" the three Texan ladies said. What shall I sing I thought? Well I am a big Ricky Martin fan! So, I said "OK, I will go on stage and sing a Ricky Martin song for you!" "Great lee, thanks!" All three girls said smiling. On to the stage, I jumped singing the song "Livin' la vida loca!" Well, not only was I singing top-notch. But two of the women I had been talking to suddenly jumped onto the stage with me. As they came over the Texan beauties started to put American dollars down my trousers. "Ooh!" I said, then I carried on singing. "She'll push and pull you down, livin, la, viva, lova!!" After fi nishing the song I had a big round of applause. Th en, "Th ank you!" I said to the crowd! Next it was more fun and joy with these girls. Th ey were defi antly women I can tell you that, I shall say no more!

Time Please

Next day, 1ˢᵗ May 1999, I went out to see where one of Senator Edward Moore Kennedy's brothers. President John Fitzgerald Kennedy had been assassinated in Deally Plaza of Dallas.

Firstly, I toured the Texas book depository on Elm Street and the Grassy Knoll where on November 22, 1963, the Texas School Book Depository building had been the focus of world shock, grief, and outrage when President John F. Kennedy was assassinated. Twenty-six years later, John F. Kennedy and the Memory of a Nation opened on the building's sixth fl oor, where signifi cant evidence was found. Well using nearly 400 photographs, 45 minutes of documentary fi lms, and artifacts, this exhibition recreates the social and political context of the early 1960s, chronicles the assassination and its aftermath, and recognizes Kennedy's lasting impact on American culture.

Also, visitors can view huge wall-mounted photographs of the President in Berlin, Washington, and in the tragic motorcade at Dallas. Videos of the motorcade and Inaugural Address are shown. On-going exhibits are presented, such as 13 cameras in use on November 22, 1963, and the model of the assassination site prepared by the FBI for the Warren Commission in 1964.

Eventually on reaching the sixth fl oor of the library you can look through the snipers nest window over Deally Plaza.

This is supposedly from where Lee Harvey Oswald took the three shots at Kennedy.

Texas Book Depository in Dallas.

At the time of shots at 12.30pm on the afternoon of Friday 22nd November 1963, when the thirty-fi fth President John Fitzgerald Kennedy of the United States of America was assassinated. Some people say three bullets many others say four were shot at him two of these badly wounding him.

All doctors who witnessed JFK's wounds all state that the president's head was partially destroyed; they say the back right side of the president's head was missing, and that 20% of his brain was not intact.

Eventually he passed away on arriving at Parkland hospital in Dallas at the time. President John Fitzgerald Kennedy was pronounced dead at 1:04pm. Extraordinarily something happened at the time of President John F.Kennedy's assassination.

Something was recorded on the Abraham Zapruda fi lm fi fteen minutes before the limousine passed through Deally Plaza at 11 miles an hour at the time for the fi rst shooting. Th is being where one of the public named Jerry Boyd Belknap, collapsed, having an apparent grand mal epileptic seizure. Th e seizure happening at 12.18pm as the motorcade came along and passed through Deally Plaza for the shooting of Kennedy at 12.30 on November 22nd 1963.Belknap dressed in army fatigues, had an epileptic seizure that managed to draw everybody's attention. But because of the timing, the seizure resembled a diversion, to keep witnesses from noticing other things that might have been going on in the vicinity.

Bilknap later claimed to have had a history of seizures since childhood. He was picked up in Deally Plaza by an ambulance, taken to Parkland Hospital's emergency area and was subsequently forgotten about because of the mass hysteria and confusion caused by the arrival of Kennedy and Governor Connolly. Without saying anything Belknap left Parkland and took a bus back to down town Dallas. Well on visiting Deally Plaza in 1999, after seeing the book depository museum. I then walked across to a little side drive near some bushes named the Grassy knoll. Th is was supposedly another area as to where President Kennedy could have maybe been shot at as his Lincoln limousine while driving along down Elm Street past the book depository. Suddenly as walking to the Grassy Knoll I noticed a Limousine, an identical copy of the Kennedy car from 1963. So I went over and asked as to what was going on. Well after talking to the man in the car. I found out that the man was doing tours of the Kennedy assassination around Deally Plaza. So I joined a group of people in the car myself sitting in the limousine. Th en as to where Governor John Connelly had sat in the President Kennedy shooting. Limousine in Dallas 5th May 1999.

Th e Limousine took me around Dallas. Showing everybody the scenario of where Kennedy's shooting had happened. Whist also along the way I saw the prison. Where Lee Harvey Oswald had been taken and shot the next day by Jack Ruby as he came out of the prison. Funnily enough, another one of the Kennedy family named Senator Robert Francis Kennedy had also been assassinated. Th is took place shortly after midnight on 5th June, 1968 in Los Angeles, California. After winning the California primary election for the Democratic nomination for President of the United States, Robert F. Kennedy was shot as he walked through the kitchen of the Ambassador Hotel and died in the Good Samaritan Hospital twentysix hours later. Th e assassin was a twenty-four year old Palestinian immigrant named Sirhan Sirhan, who remains incarcerated for this crime as of 2010. Th e shooting was recorded on audio tape by a freelance newspaper reporter, and the aftermath was captured on fi lm. Well on 4th May 1999, after the tour in the limousine and Dallas itself. I was to leave the hotel and get a free cab back to Dallas Fort-Worth airport. Now this was where I was to fi nd something else out about the hotel. Plus also the area I had been staying at in Dallas. Well whist we drove: "Excuse me sir, you know that lady. Who was at the desk by the computer in the hotel? I mentioned to the taxi driver. "Yeah?" The cab driver said.

"Was that really a lady?" I asked. Suddenly, the driver started laughing. "Did you really think that was a woman? He said. "Have you not heard them talking? "Th ere are gay men in the hotel reception; you're staying in the gay part of Dallas."

He stated still laughing. Well I thought, now I am Ricky Martin and it has been great seeing where Kennedy has been shot. But I am glad to be getting away from the transvestite in the hotel.

High and Low

Chicago:

So next on Sunday 2nd May 1999, I got a fl ight out into Chicago.

It was now time for Great massive pizzas! Th e Chicago-style pizza is a deep-dish pizza style developed in the city. Th e pizza has a buttery crust up to three inches tall at the edge, slightly higher than the large amounts of cheese and chunky tomato sauce, acting as a large bowl. Th e term also refers to "stuff ed" pizza, another Chicago style. On Monday 3rd May of 1999, whilst still in Chicago I visited the Hancock building. Which is a 100-story, 1,127—foot[3] (344 m) tall skyscraper, in the middle of Chicago. It gave a super view of Chicago! Th e only thing was that while I was in Chicago. I found out the telephone number for the studio building to where the Jerry Springer show is made. Well I made the phone call to the studio and after asking "Is there any chance of getting a ticket for the show" Unfortunately I found out that you have to write a letter to get tickets for the show. After the tour around the city I then moved on. And on the 4th of May 1999, I went onto my next State.

This state was New York, where I went into Manhattan.

I returned to see Times Square again. And a new building called the Empire State Building along with other places such as Central Park in New York. Next I visited the Rockefeller Plaza Center I did a weather report. On 4th May 1999, to fi nish my trip of in New York, I did a helicopter tour all over Manhattan. Th is went over the Statue of Liberty, Empire State building and also the massive World trade centre. Which itself again made another very exciting trip.

Eight Diff erent States!!

Two years later, on Friday 14th April 2000, I toured the world again. On this occasion I made a one month visit to America. When arriving into the country I made quite a big tour of eight diff erent states. I started my visit, by staying with my friends Jenni and Dave in Gaithersburg of Maryland.

On Monday 17th April 2000, whilst in America I went to see Philadelphia. Th is city, lies about 80 miles (130 km) southwest of New York City It is also the largest city in Pennsylvania, sixth-most-populous city in the United States. While in the city I visited the City Hall going up to the Tower of City Hall and have a pigeon's eye view of the city. First I went to the 7th fl oor and then followed the red lines on the fl oor to the escalator that goes to 9th fl oor waiting room. Then a guard took me to the top with another elevator that leads to the observation desk which is below Penn's statue.

Two days later, after having arrived back to Dave and Jenni's in Maryland. I went on 18th April to Washington D.C. next getting the train from Woodfi eld Station in Stratford of Maryland. When arriving into Washington D.C. I went onto see Abbi my new friend who had got me the ticket of 27th April 1999. Well while visiting her she again got me a ticket. To visit the Presidents house on Pennsylvania Avenue in Washington D.C. I stood in quite a cue but eventually did a tour of the White House having some photographs taken outside to the North Portico of the White House.

Afterwards, I did more tours around the capital. Like the Washington Mail which is just outside of Capitol Hill. Th ere I also saw the Lincoln Memorial, Arlington town centre. Th en on the evening after having had a few drinks with Abbi I got the train back to Dave and Je i's.

Well something else quite interesting happened. Th is on Th ursday 20th April 2000. Because after catching another train from Shady Grove into Washington and getting off at Union Station. Well while in the capital I walked into a lady. Th is lady was the wife of a Senator of America.

Well unexpectedly "I can get you a ticket to visit Capitol Hill to save you doing all of the waiting. Also very kindly she gave me six dollars to arrange a tour of Capitol Hill. So after saying "Th ank You," I went off on the tour. Th e inside of Capitol Hill was very interesting.

Th e United States Capitol in Washington, D.C., is among the most architecturally impressive and symbolically important buildings in the world. It has housed the meeting chambers of the Senate and the House of Representatives for almost two centuries. Begun in 1793, the Capitol has been built, burnt, rebuilt, extended, and restored; today, it stands as a monument not only to its builders but also to the American people and their government.

Picture of Capitol Hill from helicopter:

As the focal point of the government's Legislative Branch, the Capitol is the centerpiece of the Capitol Campus, which includes the six principal Congressional office buildings and three Library of Congress buildings constructed on Capitol Hill in the 19th and 20th centuries.

Today, the Capitol covers a ground area of 175,170 square feet, or about 4 acres, and has a fl oor area of approximately 16-1/2 acres. Its length, from north to south, is 751 feet 4 inches; its greatest width, including approaches, is 350 feet. Its height above the base line on the east front to the top of the Statue of Freedom is 288 feet; from the basement fl oor to the top of the dome is an ascent of 365 steps. Th e building contains approximately 540 rooms and has 658 windows (108 in the dome alone) and approximately 850 doorways.Th e building is divided into fi ve levels. Th e fi rst, or ground, fl oor is occupied chiefl y by committee rooms and the spaces allocated to various congressional offi cers. Th e areas accessible to visitors on this level include the Hall of Columns, the Brumidi Corridors, the restored Old Supreme Court Chamber, and the Crypt beneath the Rotunda, where historical exhibits are presented.

Th e second fl oor holds the Chambers of the House of Representatives (in the south wing) and the Senate (in the north wing) as well as the offi ces of the congressional leadership. Th is fl oor also contains three major public areas. In the center under the dome is the Rotunda, a circular ceremonial space that also serves as a gallery of paintings and sculpture depicting signifi cant people and events in the nation's history. Th e Rotunda is 96 feet in diameter and rises 180 feet 3 inches to the canopy. Th e semicircular chamber south of the Rotunda served as the Hall of the House until 1857; now designated National Statuary Hall, it houses part of the Capitol's collection of statues donated by the states in commemoration of notable citizens. Th e Old Senate Chamber northeast of the Rotunda, which was used by the Senate until 1859, has been returned to its mid-19thcentury appearance. Th e third fl oor allows access to the galleries from which visitors to the Capitol may watch the proceedings of the House and the Senate when Congress is in session. Th e rest of this fl oor is occupied by offi ces, committee rooms, and press galleries. Th e fourth fl oor and the basement/terrace level of the Capitol are occupied by offi ces, machinery rooms, workshops, and other support areas. On Friday 21ST April 2000, after staying with Dave and Jenni it was time to move on. So off I fl ew out into Portland of Oregon, where I stayed for fi ve days with another one of my friends Mike Mele. Well while with him he took me around a few places while at last I fi nally relaxed for a bit. Well, while with him and his girlfriend. We all had plenty of pizza's at his fl at and watched television. I still went to see a few things in Portland while with Mike. Places like Lloyd Centre, University for history and the Arts Museum. Eventually I left Mike on Th ursday 27th April 2000, going back to the eastern side of America. I arrived visiting friends in West Virginia for my birthday. Whilst with them, I again did plenty more touring in the states of Washington D.C, Virginia and West Virginia. Eventually on Tuesday 2nd May 2000, I went on fl ying into Boston. Where on Wednesday 3rd May 2000. I saw an American baseball game at Fenway Park. Here the Boston Redsocks played against Detroit which ended the Boston Red Sox 4—2 Detroit. After a few days of looking around Boston I then went on Monday 8th May 2000, off into New York. While in Manhattan I got a ticket and by going across on a ferry I did a tour to the Statue of Liberty. Eventually I again returned on Th ursday 10th May 2000 back into England.

Hospital Bill!

More pleasure was to come in November of 2000, but also not quite what was to be expected. Well on Friday 3rd November 2000, I fl ew out to Los Angeles from Heathrow Airport. Unfortunately while on the plain I became very tired. But suddenly but still aware of all, I suddenly went into two very light semi conscious epileptic seizures. Luckily only slight jerking

I eventually came out of the seizure. But so what!! Let's think about the good things! I am fl ying out to America a dream achieved which we can all achieve when we try. On arriving into Los Angeles, I dropped my bags off at the hotel. Th en went off around many pubs where I suddenly meet up with some American lads and having a great night out. So we stayed in this nightclub having a laugh with many American women. Th ese girls loved my accent so until 6.00am the next morning we all stayed and had a laugh together. Th e next day I got up and Los Angeles was roasting. I saw Mann's Chinese Th eatre. But unfortunately while there I ended up having another epileptic seizure in the town and ended up in hospital. I was not too happy. I was fully aware of what was going on just like the plane while having the seizure.

Eventually I came out of the hospital and went back to the hotel. Th e next day getting up still loving America! But not understanding how this country can be so far ahead in the world and have no free health service. Still I carried on touring around. I went into Santa Monica, for the day. To which I eventually visited quite a few times throughout my visit. Later on the night I returned to my hotel in Los Angeles again back around the pubs. It was karaoke night!

Th is is where Ricky Martin again came onto the stage. I went up onto the stage and sang a few of my favourite songs. Again being told I was very good. Then after chatting to more American chicks and seeing more sites. Places such as Wiltshire by the Metro train. Later into the week I did a helicopter tour. Th is was a night tour!

Across the sky of Los Angles at night it is beautiful with so much colour from the lights!

Also I had the honour of meeting characters Mickey Mouse, Trigger, Igor and Whinny the Pooh. Th is time Whinny the Pooh did not go to the toilet. Th en for the last few days I toured around diff erent parts of L.A. and around Santa Monica.

Th roughout the nights, I would visit diff erent pubs and nightclubs meeting some very nice people. Suddenly after talking to a lovely lady named Alison from one night club in L.A. We would meet up for the last few days of my visit.

She really wanted to start dating me as I with her but not able to because of diff erent countries. Unfortunately my trip eventually came to an end. Another interesting story! My health again trying to stop me! But it never will! Ending up in hospital! Having seizures! I met some lovely people in California. Seeing some fantastic things from ground and from the sky in the helicopter tour!

I might not have my health but determination and confi dence I have and that I shall always have and I am proud of this! I want to help people to build there's!

Unexpectedly though a few days later after arriving back into Staff ord of the West Midlands in the United Kingdom. I received a letter through the door. Th is was from the Los Angeles hospital where I had ended up due to the epileptic seizure. Th e bill to pay was for me spending a few hours in this hospital. I could not believe it this is one of the big problems in America. Th is is that America does not have a free health service. Luckily before I had fl own out to Los Angeles I had made sure that I was covered in case anything happened to me while I was out in California. So the insurance company paid for the bill that had come from the Los Angeles hospital.

Hot stuff!!

Well on Tuesday 17th April 2001, I fl ew out to America.For my thirtieth birthday, my love was and will always be there for the country. Obviously making sure I was covered with health insurance. In case what happened in Los Angeles did not happen on this visit to the United States of America. I fl ew out from Heathrow Airport in London onto Washington Dulles Airport of America. On arriving I got a train from the airport eventually to meet my friends Dave and Jennie at Shady Grove in Maryland. On Friday 20th April 2001, I did a helicopter tour around Washington D.C. Next day I started going around on diff erent trains around Maryland and Washington D.C. Eventually on Tuesday 22nd April, I fl ew into Honolulu. Where I stayed in an area named Wakiki. On Wednesday 25th April I did a tour of Pearl Harbour. We were taken around the area as to where the terrible bombing had happened. At 7.55am on Sunday 7 December 1941, the fi rst of two waves of Japanese aircraft began their deadly attack on the US Pacifi c Fleet, moored at Pearl Harbour on the Pacifi c island of Oahu. Within two hours, fi ve battleships had been sunk, another 16 damaged, and 188 aircraft were destroyed. Only luck saved three US aircraft carriers, usually stationed at Pearl Harbour but assigned elsewhere on the day. Th e attacks killed under 100 Japanese but over 2,400 Americans, with another 1,178 injured. On my visit it was certainly not a place to be for people who do not like hot weather. It must have been about 26 degrees and very humid. I went on the hotel sun bed after buying some cheep sun cream from a local shop for myself.

What happened? Th e next day after sunbathing for this one hour the inside of my legs well! Th ey were bright red! Luckily this though was after I had celebrated my thirtieth birthday where I had a great time. On the 26th April, this the day before my birthday I was in a local pub of Honolulu talking to two Canadian girls. Suddenly "Is that food free? I asked these girls. Th en "Yes, go and ask that man over there!" they said. So I thought OK why not! I went over "Excuse me sir is the food over there free it is my birthday tomorrow could I have some!" I said to a man.

Th en "Well it costs $50.00 but I will let you have what you want for $40.00 as it is your birthday." "OK cheers." I said. And over I went getting some food and on the night I joined in the club going around the pub crawl. Most people were Canadian. I stayed with these great looking Canadian girls. We had drinks and did plenty of dancing throughout the night well over midnight to start a great birthday on the 27th April 2001 for me.

Well on waking up the next day. I got ready and went into Waikiki and decided for my birthday after a great time the night before to do a helicopter tour over the city. Magic taking some sound photo's again another very warm day beautiful sky's and blue sea. So that was the start of a super thirtieth birthday.

Th en next on my birthday there was another funny story on the night this being where I met up with another man who had come to Oahu visiting Honolulu for a holiday. Well we decided to nightclub on the night of my birthday together. But not quite night club as you would think. Th is because it was a strip bar in Honolulu, I had a think and so off we both went. I had never been in a nuddy bar before and it is my birthday so why not for a laugh so in we went. Well it is certainly something you will never forget on entering. Th ere was a bar just like anywhere else inside to get drinks.

Next in the middle you had a stage, which looked like a small round high dance fl oor. On the stage this person a lady was dancing by herself with pants on but no brier. At the same time there was this man below with a long piece of rope. On numerous occasions he would put this dollar of some form connected to some rope down her pants. Th is lady would constantly turn around and give him a big kiss. Suddenly after she turned back around and carried on dancing on this stage to other people in the room. So many times he would then pull the rope out and then push it back down her pants again. Th en the lady turned giving him another kiss. Either she must have been a bit thick or had big pants!

Th en at the end of the show sitting at a table with a drink by myself a lady, not the one from the stage though came over to me. "Would you like to go upstairs for forty dollars." She said. Now I knew this was not for just a drink. "No you are OK thank you; I respect you for who you are."

I said. Th en she gave me a big kiss and went off. Well on Wednesday 2nd May 2001, I left Wakiki of Oahu in Hawaii. Next going on into San Francisco where I visited another of my friends in America. While staying in San Francisco I had a few walks around and across the Golden Gate Bridge and then fl ew back into the United Kingdom on 1st May 2001.

CHAPTER SIX

FLASHING LIGHTS

After ten years of working at Stephen Glovers Industrial Company. I left the factory and started to get involved in other subjects. I had a think! Lee, how about sports photography! Who with? How? Th en suddenly I realised! Th e Albion! I love my soccer, and thought let's study soccer as my project! Well who can I and how do I contact the soccer club. To get permission to take photographs. Radio stations! Yeah! I thought. Well how about contacting them to fi nd out, who I should speak to at West Bromwich Albion Football Club.

Well talking on the radio, is something I regularly do whether about medical, football or some other world issues. I telephoned Radio West Midlands in Birmingham asking to speak to Paul Franks. I spoke to him live on a show "Hi Paul, who should I contact about doing photography with the Albion?" I asked. "Contact Dr John Evans the secretary at the club for permission." Franksy said. So, off I went hoping to do action photography in 1998. Well I did this, and wrote to Dr Evans in September 1998 about photographing a game. He suddenly wrote back to me saying. Yes, it was

O.K. to photograph at West Bromwich Albion football club. Amazing and disbelief! What a fantastic experience and honour!" I thought.

Photo I took at West Bromwich Albion football club in May 1999.

Well along came Saturday May 1st 1999, and it was West Brom against Bury! One of the hardest things about taking sport pictures with impact is getting close to the subject in the fi rst place. It's almost impossible to take shots professionally if or when taking them through wire fences or from a packed grandstand.

Also asking the stewards on the day will usually get you nowhere either. This even though, I was sitting behind the advertisement board on the football pitch towards the goal. Suddenly half way through the game I suddenly heard, "Excuse me sir can you turn your fl ash off please!" from some steward. Well, typical of me with my camera fl ash shooting off wild. I did not realise you were unable to have a camera light or fl ash shooting off in the ground.

So off the fl ash went and I carried on doing the photography. Albion eventually beat Bury. The game finishing: West Bromwich Albion 1-0 Bury. One great experience! With unexpectedly more photography to come! Plus I also controlled myself amazingly when the Baggies scored.

Bobby Robson & Me.

A few days later, excited again I contacted West Bromwich Albion over the telephone. Well what could I say? I thought. So I mentioned as to if I can carry on doing photography with the Albion. Suddenly "Yes you can carry on doing the photography at West Bromwich Albion football club." I was told.

So every day just before the game, I would go off into the ticket office to pick up my Press ticket. The Holy Grail in sports photography is the press pass. A photographer with one of these little beauties gains free access to the venue, and can expect to be centimetres, not meters, away from the action on the sports field.

Kings College Hospital

In 2001, after returning, from my thirtieth birthday tour of America. I received a telephone call and letter. Th ese were from Kings College Hospital in London. Th e telephone call was from Dr Nandini Mullati my neurologist and others from my surgeon Professor Polkey of 1992.

Unfortunately, the letter and telephone calls. I had received were not for me to go out enjoying myself. Th ey were for more EEG tests at Kings College Hospital in London.

So in July 2001, off I went into Kings College. At the time just expecting some form of EEG, MRI or CAT scans. Th is time though it was to be a little bit more serious than that. Well, yes it was for tests, but a little more serious. Because it was electrodes, that were to be glued to my head for an EEG test. Th ey were planted onto my scalp. Glued to my head like as in late 1989. Th en my brain's activity was studied on machines by neurologists for a few days. Th is to see if medical surgeons had any new identifi cation as to which part of the lobe the electrical activity was coming. We all knew it was in the left temporal lobe area of the nervous system in my brain.

But as if the operation wasn't painful enough on 22nd October 1992. I went under the knife again. Suddenly, while in discussion "Lee you can have the operation, but you have to stay awake, so think about it." My doctors mentioned to me as they thought they'd identifi ed the problem.

Well I thought they were joking. Me being the comedian I am. But I suddenly realised after looking at them again that they were not Soon we went on to discuss the success, and also the consequences there may be in surgery. "What are the risks in the operation?" I asked. Th en "Lee, there is a chance that if something goes wrong. "You may lose the site out in the corner of your eyes. "Maybe your mouth and tongue also slurring as you talk. "But these will both come back. "Th en the same could happen as of your fi rst operation. "For instance you could become paralysed down the right hand side of your body." Th is Professor Polkey and Dr Nandini Mulatti both stated. Th en "You will not be cutting my head open like you did last time, will you Professor Polkey?" I next mentioned. Suddenly "No, no, Lee we just insert a little needle into the centre of your scull, and burn the tumour out near the damaged part of your brain." Professor Polkey stated. Th en still somehow smiling, "I will still be as good looking after the operation won't I Doctor Mullatti, ah?" I asked. Th en "Of course you will lee!" laughing and smiling as well back to me Dr Mullatti said. Well it took me about fi ve minutes to make my decision in the meeting of 2001. Well! "If it's going to get rid of these dam tingling sensations in my stomach, and bring my health back then I'll go for the operation." I said. We then fi nished the discussion.

So 1st August 2001, arrived and the procedures of the operation came. Removing the brain tumour involved me sitting for four hours while surgeons carried out surgery.

Complex brain surgery!

I was rolled into the operating theatre. Th en suddenly after the fi rst minute or two I felt an injection go into the back of my scull. Suddenly I felt the pain of an injection all over the back of my head. I assumed this was the anaesthetic, which I could feel, myself, by now starting to pray it would stop any pain that could come.

Th e shock was when surgeons drilled into the back of my skull, and I felt the tools. Th e pain was horrible to start with. I thought the needle was a drilling machine. What was happening? Well the needle had been going into the top back centre of my head. Th en the anaesthetics started to take eff ect. I was absolutely terrifi ed.

Th e anaesthetics seemed to take eff ect about one hour later! I felt nothing apart from the tingling stomach sensations. Of which I had to explain to all of the doctors throughout the operation about during the operation.

Suddenly "One is starting now!" I regularly shouted and then my voice would rise. Th is just like I constantly had been trying to explain as a child. I prayed in my mind please get rid of these "Horrible things!" Th e surgeons and his team tried to reassure me as much as possible but it was terrifying.

I just gritted my teeth all throughout the operation.

As it carried on, now I was still consciously explaining myself. To the surgeons when I was having any tingling nerve sensations in my stomach. Or at the same time also an epileptic seizure. Th is of which regularly happened while I was in the operating theatre.

For this reason I had to explain about the tingling sensations. So they could try and identify the tumour problem. I remember the last moment of the operation "Dr Mullatt, Dr Mullatti one is starting now an Aura!!" Suddenly a tingling sensation started. Please let them stop I prayed!

Suddenly counting half way and then to nine the tingling stopped! Suddenly my voice did not rise or anything.

Well what has happened, I was fully conscious. And I did not have a giggling sensation, expecting my voice tone to rise. It was shocking! A dramatic experience! Four hours and the operation had fi nished. I was so relieved! Now I have gone through brain surgery asleep and awake! Th e fi rst time waking my head was twice its size. Th e second time I was to stay awake for a drill to start in the back of my head.

As we went out of the surgery the fi rst thing I asked was

"Can I ring my mum to tell her I am OK please?" I then telephoned mum with the great news. "Mum it is over I am alright and they have got rid of these dam tingling stomach sensations!"

It's fantastic not to have the sensations any more now I could relax without getting frustrated because of them.

Th e seizures were not cured, but the surgery very much helped the form of epileptic seizure. Suddenly they were not so severe, only my eyes would twitch along with a few muscle spasms on the left side of my body. Th is would go on for a second maybe or up to twenty minutes. But the main thing is then and now I am fully aware of the seizures.

It was thought that I had a developmental abnormality in the brain and that removing this damaged part could improve the epilepsy.

At the time of my operation, I needed to be conscious, because the area causing the epilepsy was close to a vital part of the brain, which is used for breathing, sleeping, feeding and memory.

Talking normally during the operation was vital then the surgeon knew that I was all right. But the general epileptic seizure decreased in amount and severity.

When I came out of the operation my head was killing me and I had to take tablets, but the next morning it was relatively OK.

Another thing as well is that my short—term memory returned almost immediately after the surgery and, better still and as mentioned the epilepsy had very much improved.

I insert my discharge summaries from the second operation. Then I discuss my returning home and recovery from the operation

Discharge summery

Lee has a long and complicated history of epilepsy and had undergone a left temporal lobotomy for an apparent focal seizure onset about ten years ago. Since then, fortunately, technology has advanced and very high quality MRI scanning had demonstrated a very small lesion is known within the hypothalamus. Such a lesion is known rarely to be a cause of intractable epilepsy, often of its gelastic quality (that is, seizures involving laughing). Open surgery for these lesions is extremely diffi cult and it was decided to attempt a new technique of depth electrodes, including an electrode into the lesion. Th is confi rmed epileptogenic activity typical gelestic attack. Having successfully proven seizure onset from this site, we then proceeded to a thermocoagulation of the lesion under local anaesthetic. Post-operatively Lee had no new defi cits and indeed his seizures and aura frequencies were very dramatically reduced. He had no new defi cits and indeed his seizure and aura frequency were very dramatically reduced. He had one noctural myocolomic attack before discharged directly home and he will be followed up by Dr Mullatti in her clinic in the next few weeks.

Mr Richard Selway
Super Photography

After all of the returning to and from hospitals. It was time to decide and think. Th is about my ambitions and dreams in life. By now having undergone my second operation at Kings College in London 2001. Would I maybe do more action photography? Maybe tour around the world again?

Th is could be while still taking Ricky Martin off in pubs and clubs around places while still living at my fl at in Staff ord.

Well in August 2001, to begin with. I started taking shots by going back on into photography at West Bromwich Albion Football Club. There were to still be many more great shots in black and white fi lm from everywhere to come around the stadium.

Amazingly even though taking and doing so many good photographs. Th ere was something else achievable. It was nothing to do with pictures but more to do with the supporting of the club. Basically what would I do if the Albion scored? Would I stay quite or maybe jump up and start going wild like the crowd behind me.

Well strangely enough on Sunday March 25th 2001, while West Bromwich Albion were playing Tranmere Rovers. After starting to captivate my photography at the West Brom soccer match. Dramatically Bob Taylor the man every Baggies fan supports and worshiped scored again!

Him being one of the special men I had met on my twenty first birthday! Now, I had done so well staying quiet after Super Bob scored his fi rst goal in the 39th minute for the Albion. Well-done Lee! I thought. But suddenly West Brom scored again in the 62nd minute! Of course who was it as well? Super Bob Taylor again! But on this one occasion getting a little too excited. Who joined in? Well of course it was me jumping up!! Of which was not a good idea.

Especially being so close to the pitch with security, police and another 30,000 people around me in the crowd. Th ey were all well behind me in the stands. Celebrating, cheering and going crazy! Suddenly, "Lee sit down quick you'll get chucked out." photographers around advised me. Luckily I sat down very fast and carried on doing my photography as to not get into trouble. Th en just letting the 30,000 Albion supporters carry on celebrating around me in the stadium. Luckily after this my emotions were to be well controlled. Th is even in a local derby with Birmingham City, Super Bob scored another one of his many goals! Now so much had been learnt. With some very interesting photography work at the soccer team I love.

Taking photographs was super with West Bromwich Albion from 1999 to 2003 seasons. Th en and now I am still taking many more great shots in black and white fi lm from all areas around. I developed many camera fi lms at home in Staff ord or maybe still in Wolverhampton.

Th roughout the work, I would go into the developing dark rooms in Wolverhampton and Stafford to make many great pictures. I would put the developed fi lms into a developer (Fix), for fi ve minutes in liquids which brings the picture up. Not letting any light into the room was very important due to the good quality of my picture. Because if too much light appeared on the picture then it would be damaged. One interesting subject was that while developing and designing the pictures. In the darkroom with some usages of diff erent fi lters. Th ese are like small square size pieces of plastic. Extraordinarily the fi lters would lighten or darken the image quality amazingly. Th roughout the photography I did at West Bromwich Albion football club for three seasons. I had the honour of meeting some very famous soccer players and managers.

Some of these people were Bobby Robson, Trevor Francis, David Platt and Kevin Keegan. Th e most memorable story about meeting people was the Kevin Keegan story because something very interesting happened. Well, I wrote early in the week before the soccer match between West Bromwich Albion and Manchester City. For permission to meet Kevin when he visited Th e Hawthorns home of the Albion. Well the secretary of Kevin Keegan emailed me saying get to the game early and I could then meet him. So Saturday 8th September 2001, on I went taking Th omas my cousin to the game. Now while there I went into the Press department. At the same time Th omas sat in the crowd until I got him permission to come into the press lounge department after the game. Well before the start of the match I managed to get a picture with Kevin Keegan. Th en I started the photography of the game to which fi nished West Bromwich Albion 4-0 Manchester City. Kevin Keegan & me on Saturday 8th September 2001.

After the game, I managed to take Th omas into the press department. To see if he could come and meet Kevin. But suddenly "Mr Keegan is very upset with his players and has kicked them out of the ground. "Before changing we do not think he will be coming in to be interviewed." Security guards said. Everybody waited while Gary Megson the West Brom manager was interviewed. Th en suddenly around ten minutes or so later Kevin came in. On coming into the press department he answered one question then stormed out. As he went "Could you sign this book for Th omas?" I asked. Which he very kindly stopped to do the only thing though was as he got to the book for signing. I had not given him a pen of which he was not very happy about. Th en I gave Kevin Keegan the pen and he signed the books for Tom and me.

Th roughout all of this I eventually managed to pass my City and Guilds second grade in Photography taken at Wolverhampton of the West Midlands in the United Kingdom of 2003. Well with great success after passing my course I was pleasantly invited back into another game for photography at West Bromwich Albion football club. Th is was photographing on the player I still worshiped testimonial Super Bobby Taylor.

Palm Trees

On Wednesday 14th November 2001, I started touring around again in between the photography. To start with I flew out to Miami of Florida. While out in Miami I stopped by South Beach. Where there were many Palm beaches and palm trees everywhere. While around the sunny Miami hot beaches on evenings I also went around many of the pubs and clubs.

Eventually on Wednesday 21st November 2001, I fl ew off into San Diego of California. While at San Diego in November 2001, I could not believe American people. Th ey still thought as usual that I am from Australia, New Zealand or Ireland. Funny because in San Diego a Mexican lady also thought I was from Russia. Well I went into hysterics! Also interesting was when visiting Tijuana of Mexico on Sunday 25th November and also Tuesday 27th November 2001. It took seconds to get into Mexico but hours to get back into America. Unfortunately I eventually had to fl y back on Wednesday 28th November 2001 into the United Kingdom.

Crystal ball

Well on Friday 27th December 2002, I decided to fl y out again to New York. Th is time looking forward to a celebration for New Years Eve in Manhattan. Where I stayed in a hotel just around the corner from Times Square.

Times Square is a major commercial intersection in the borough of Manhattan in New York City, at the junction of Broadway and Seventh Avenue. Stretching from West 42nd to West 47th Streets. The extended Times Square area, also called the Theater District, consists of the blocks between Sixth and Eighth Avenues from east to west, and West 40th and West 53rd Streets from south to north, making up the western part of the commercial area of Midtown Manhattan.

Suddenly whilst walking along, I began talking about Times Square to a gentleman. "Get to the Square early you will not see anything otherwise!" the man said. So on Tuesday 31ˢᵗ December 2002, I went on into Times Square at around 4.30pm where I stayed and just waited for the celebration show.

As New Years Eve came, I had eaten my sandwiches and cans of coke. But by then it became quite shocking. Due to the amount of security guards around on the roads. Plus also having myself managed to take food and cans through onto the street. This all after being tested while in the queue with crowds now in Times Square.

Well, along with millions of other people from around the world. I was to end up having a super time in Times Square. An estimated 750,000 people gathered in midtown Manhattan to watch the famous Times Square Crystal ball drop. The exterior of the Ball is illuminated by 168 Philips Halogena Brilliant Crystal light bulbs, exclusively engineered for the New Year's Eve Ball to enhance the Waterford crystal. Th e interior of the Ball is illuminated by 432 Philips Light Bulbs (208 clear, 56 red, 56 blue, 56 green, and 56 yellow), and 96 high-intensity strobe lights, which together create bright bubbling bursts of colour. Th e 696 lights and 90 rotating pyramid mirrors are computer controlled, enabling the Ball to produce a state-of-the-art light show of eyedazzling colourful patterns and a spectacular kaleidoscope eff ect atop One Times Square.

Eventually on the night, Christopher Reeve along with his wife Dana were to come along on into Times Square.

Th en to the let down the Crystal ball for New Years Eve of 2002. Christopher Reeve joined Mayor Michael Bloomberg to signal the descent of the 1,070-pound Waterford crystal ball. Police offi cers were in full force everywhere at the gatherings, but few disturbances were reported. Unbelievably for this New Years Eve in Times Square, sharpshooters were stationed on roofs, undercover offi cers mixed with the crowd, and some offi cers carried metal detectors. Then everybody stood in Times Square until midnight. Eventually mid-night came and everybody started to count. Ten, nine, eight, seven, six, fi ve, four, three, two, one!! Suddenly the crystal Ball lit up and tunes of confetti came down all over everybody in the centre of Times Square.

Bing Drinking

Th ere are two questions that have to be considered when the question of alcohol use and epilepsy comes up. One is the effect that alcohol could have on the medicines used to control seizures. Alcohol can be dangerous when mixed with sedative drugs, such as phenobarbital, and can cause coma, or even death. The other question is whether the alcohol itself will cause seizures.

Large amounts of alcohol are thought to raise the risk of seizures and may even cause them. When you drink alcohol, it temporarily reduces seizures for a few hours, but then increases the chances of having seizures as the alcohol leaves your body. Th us, people who drink heavily, even though they may not have epilepsy, may experience seizures after periods of binge drinking.

However when it comes to "social drinking"— that is, having one or two drinks during an evening — there seems to be a lot of individual variation. Some people with epilepsy are not aff ected, and some are. A drink as part of a large meal is less likely to cause a seizure than a drink on an empty stomach.

Check with your doctor before deciding on your own alcohol use. Be sure to ask about the kind of medicine you are taking and how it might react with beer, wine, or hard liquor. Th ere is roughly the same amount of alcohol in a glass of wine, a bottle of beer and a shot of liquor.

After spending the New Years Eve night at Times Square in 2003. I went onto stay with my friend Terri. I visited New Jersey which is seconds away from Manhattan itself. He took me into an area named Princeton in Indiana which was to make it my seventieth American state seen since 94. While still on my visit in New York on Sunday 5th January 03. I did my super helicopter tour over Manhattan. Th en after spending a few more days in New York I fl ew back to England on Monday 06th January 03.

Whitecaps!!!

In June of 03, I fl ew out to Canada. While there I stayed in Surrey which is just outside of Vancouver in the area of British Columbia. While there I spent two weeks visiting some very interesting places. Such as

Anderson Lake Park and Granville Island. At Anderson Lake Park and at the Granville Island you can see a great view of Vancouver: Next Hudson's Bay River. Also I saw Gas Town it was amazing I did a fl oat plane tour on Th ursday 30th May 03 in Vancouver. My favourite time of my vacation out in Canada was on Friday 30th May 03. Th is was where I went to see Canadian Soccer. Th is soccer match was at the Swangard Stadium which is located at the corner of Kingsway and Boundary in Central Park of Burnaby, British Columbia. At the soccer game I watched Vancouver Whitecaps play Montreal Impact where the match fi nished Vancouver Whitecaps 1—0 Montreal Impact.

Meat Vancouver Whitecaps.

Canadian soccer is a little diff erent to European soccer If after ninety minutes the game is still all square on a level score. Th en the teams will automatically play extra time. Strangely though the game is played until one of the two teams scores. But if nobody scores in the extra thirty minutes of extra-time. Th en that is when the game becomes a draw.

CHAPTER SEVEN

HOWDY LEE

Well before Sunday 1st June 03, after returning from Canada something very interesting had happened. Th is was while going around Staff ord's town centre in the middle of the West Midlands in England. Unexpectedly while walking into a local bread shop in mid-April 03 I started to have a talk with a lady. Well as everybody paid for the food "Where are you from?" I asked. Th en "I am from Poland." the lady said. Well after mentioning all about my polish family connections. She suddenly mentioned about a Polish club held on Sunday nights. So in late May 2003, I had made my fi rst visit to this polish club in Staff ord. On going into the club it was very exciting. Because there were so many Polish people from the Second World War. Along also with people like me who were in some way also related to a Polish family. Well while at one of the Sunday parties something hilarious happened. Th is was while I did not understand the slightest word of polish "Czesc!" "Ah!" I thought. Th at is polish for "Hello". Well throughout all of this I laughed along with everybody. At the same time trying to concentrate on learning the Polish language. Suddenly eye to eye!! A Polish lady and I started to look at each other. Well neither the polish lady nor me could make any sense of each other due to the languages. Eventually I started to make regular appearances to the club.

Very interesting, I still tried to discuss and talk to this lady about myself. Eventually I was to fi nd out that this ladies name was Natalie. Regularly we still tried to understand and speak to ea Then on we went into the 80's you had starting in 83-17 with NBC was the A-Team is an action adventure series about a fictional group of ex-United States Army Special Forces personnel who work as soldiers of fortune, coming ni regularly more comig along was ch other by going over to a map of Poland in the Polish club's room. Th roughout all of this trying to grasp my Birmingham accent did not help either. Th is still while Natalie was showing me where she and her family were from in Poland.

Th en in August of 2003, Natalie and I along with a group of friends from the polish club went into Stafford town centre on a Saturday night out around the pubs. That was the start of a very close relationship between Magda and me. Next in the story I will talk about another story and afterwards go back to my living in Staff ord.

Dozed off!!!

Well on Saturday 27th December 03, I went out again for New Years Eve to New York. But this was not quite to be the start of my trip that I was expecting. I will now discuss the story of my unexpected seizure. This was to be while on a Lufthansa plane. That at the time was half way across the Atlantic Ocean. Unbelievably we suddenly returned back to the United Kingdom just because of me. Should I feel honoured or angry!

So on the Saturday, oh dear! I suddenly started to fall asleep on the plane with Lufthansa. Th is a German air company as we fl ew from Manchester to New York. Th en as I dozed off I jumped out of my sleep and went into an epileptic seizure. My eyes twitching and left arm jerking for a minute. I was fully in control of all just in need to sit calm and relaxed until it stopped. But suddenly airhostesses came over "Are you OK sir!" they said. Well, "Yes no problem thank you, I am having an epileptic seizure. But don't worry it will stop in a minute." I stated. Th e airhostesses did not seem to understand a word I was talking about. Unbelievably half way across the Atlantic Ocean, and on our way out to Manhattan the plane turned around. Because I was having an epileptic seizure! Well unexpectedly arriving back into London there was much frustration!

Eventually there is a lot more to explain and write about in this story. Like my fantastic New Year's Eve in Times Square along with a wee, wee in a lucozade bottle while the police walk around with guns. Plus many, many more stories in my diff erent twenty USA States visited. But this plane on returning was not landing into J.F. Kennedy airport of Manhattan. It was returning back into an English airport. But suddenly on arriving back into London of England an ambulance and doctors came over to look at me! I started to get a little frustrated. Well "Sir we will have to take you off!" the paramedics said. "I am OK!" I said back. Eventually I was taken off after having my heartbeat and blood tested. At the time everybody was performing as though I had been dying.

Well, I spoke to my mum on the telephone very unhappy, got my suitcases. Suddenly then to end the shock "We cannot get you a fl ight without a letter from your doctor."

Lufthansa said. Luckily, I was then told that British Airways would fl y me into America from Manchester the next day. So I got a taxi up to Manchester. Mum had booked me a hotel room by the airport in Manchester. Now then after fi nally calming down it was time for something else.

Th is was because I suff er terrible with travel sickness. So on the way up to Manchester, by now looking white in the face. I had to stop at mum's house in Staff ord. I walked in throwing up sick at her house. Eventually on Saturday 27th December, I ended up staying at mum and Howard's house for the night.

Next day, Sunday 28th December 03, Howard very kindly gave me a lift up to Manchester airport. Eventually when arriving into Manchester I went to the airport. Th en I fi nally fl ew out to Manhattan with British Airways.

When arriving into Manhattan of America I had a fantastic time! My friend Dave from New Jersey took me to see so many new places. First we went to see a game of American football. Th e game fi nished the New York Giants 24—37 South Carolina. Next day we went up to New York on a few occasions before staying there for New Years Eve. Th roughout and around all of this, I eventually spent New Year's Eve in Times Square. A great experience! Most pubs are both restaurants and bars all in one, I went to Pubs on 8th avenue 45th street. Th is being where my hotel was and clubs around Manhattan such as the "Rainbow Room" on 49th Street and 5th to 6th Avenue's then also New York City's largest nightclub named "Exit" which is on 56th street 11th and 12th avenues. In all clubs and pubs I had a really super time with people there. Times Square which is on 7th avenue between 45th street has much colour at night. On Tuesday 31st December, 2002 I could see the crowds starting to build up. So like the year before I made sure I was there early. Last year it was 4.30.pm but in 04 I was there for 12.30pm. Now to be standing in by the gates on the pavements towards the roads of Times Square. By then I had started talking to a couple from Memphis in Tennessee. Th en at about 4.00pm that is when the police started to appear. Talking to the crowds and moving people around me. We were eventually all taken back onto the street just off Times Square to be checked?

Police were checking everybody for guns, bombs and all. Eventually after having my bags checked and returned by security I went through. No alcohol was allowed in but somehow cans of coke.

Th ey got in around the police to drink. Well who was it carrying them in his bag. Off cause it was me. Which I was to eventually pay back for on the night. As all started to close in everybody and everywhere went very quiet. Suddenly a big street party started from around 7.00pm. Where people unexpectedly came along everywhere passing around big hats. Th ese were long red hats, which also would lighten up.

As the night darkened suddenly the streets lit up! Amazing lights in fantastic colours! At 8.00pm well this was time for the sandwich and cans of coke for my tea. Later though oh dear I was unexpectedly in need of the toilet. I thought what shall I do? The shops are close but there are some the other side of the fences by the roads.

Unfortunately if I go to a local shop, I will not get my place back because there are so many people here. Basically same as an airport standing in lines and so on. Suddenly while standing and talking to a man from Florida, "I am busting for the restroom!!" I said. Th en "Looks like you have paid for drinking that coke!" said the man. Next I then started standing crossing my legs with a little more need for the restroom or toilet as we call it over here in England.

An hour or so later time by then reaching 9.30pm I was about to wet myself. But suddenly the man from Tampa Bay in Florida, "Th ere is a man over there with a big bottle letting people have a pee in for $5.00." he said. Eventually I needed to go over and ask. So "I hear your giving a lucazade bottle around for $5.00." I said. He gave me the bottle already half full. When "You can have for free!" he mentioned "Just throw it away when finished!" then he finished. So I walked off holding this lucazade bottle. So, lee how the hell am I going use this, I thought. While looking at the security men with big machine guns I managed to walk back to where I had been standing before by this man from Florida. Th en, "You can have a pee so the police will not see you, but do not put anything over my coat. He said. Next he put his coat around me. I then had a pee but it went all over his coat. I was amazed he was not upset! After this we had a great night laughing joking and all.

Eventually Cindy Lauper just after 11.00pm did a three song show. It was super matching her singing on stage in Times Square. Th en at midnight 10,9,8,7,6,5,4,3,2,1,0, Happy New Year!! the crowd all shouted. As confetti fell in Times Square and the crystal ball lit up. I automatically joined in with the celebrations!!

On returning back to my hotel after all of the excitement in Times Square. I toured many other places around the area of New York. On Friday 2nd January 04, I did more touring around. Visiting Delaware, by Amtrac which is the train going into Wilmington. Delaware is the banking part of the USA. It was very funny because there accent was very broad. While around nobody seemed to understand a word I was saying.

People there seemed to come from northern and southern parts of the USA. Next day it was onto Connecticut, this is the state above New York. I stopped off in New Haven in Norwich a gambling centre of Connecticut. Th en on I went visiting Philadelphia for a day. New Years Eve in Times Square 03.

Eventually after a few other bits and pieces the two weeks were fi nished. But I was about to pack my bags when I suddenly realised "Shit I was supposed to have fl ew back to the United Kingdom yesterday!" So excitement and shock. Due to me missing my fl ight but funny because Lufthansa were supposed to get me there originally. But eventually I got back to Britain with another company on Tuesday 6th January. Very interesting after having been on another visit to Manhattan of New York. Celebrating New Years Eve in Times Square!

Cannon 500.

So in came August of 03, I was now back in England. Eventually having fi nished the photography at West Bromwich Albion. I will always have many special memory from the action work. That memory of course is not so much about the meeting of sports players but more about the Tranmere Rovers game when I was jumping up and down on Super Bob Taylor scoring that goal.

Afterwards I regularly used my Cannon 500 camera with the 500.m.m.lens. Plus also photographs maybe still with 1600 speed in black and white fi lm for fast action pictures. Fast speed fi lm helps with the action pictures for good developed focus in the picture. Th is meaning the more pixels there are in a fi lm the better the photograph will be when developed. Later photographs plus fi lms were made and I went on to sell the diff erent action photographs to people around the West Midlands.

After and around that I was still dating Natalie. Eventually after meeting up with each other it was time to go a little further. So after having made my visit to New York it was time for a new life. Because Magda and I started living with each other on Tuesday 13th January 2004. By then I was still trying to work out her language of which was quite diffi cult but I was getting there. "Czesc Natalie, Jak sie masz?" I would say. This means "Hello, how are you?" in Polish. So Magda and me were by now starting to pick each others words up.

Soon on Friday 09th May 04, I was to make my fi rst visit to Poland. Where I was to visit Eva and Maciek they were the mother and father of Natalie While making the visit to Poland I saw places such as Krakow.

Th is is the second largest and one of the oldest cities in Poland. While there I visited places such as Wawel Castle. Th e Gothic Wawel Castle in Cracow in Poland was built at the behest of Casimir III the Great and consists of a number of structures situated around the central courtyard.

In the 14th century it was rebuilt by Jogaila and Jadwiga of Poland.

A few days later I went onto Auschwitz. Th is was where from 1940 until 1945 many Jewish and Polish people were gassed and tortured by Nazi Germany. It was a network of concentration and extermination camps built and operated in Polish areas annexed by Nazi Germany during the Second World War. It was the largest of the German concentration camps, consisting of Auschwitz I (the Stammlager or base camp); Auschwitz II-Birkenau (the Vernichtungslager or extermination camp); Auschwitz III-Monowitz, also known as Buna-Monowitz (a labor camp); and 45 satellite camps.

When hearing the story of what Nazi German solders did to Jewish and Polish people. It was quite frightening to think how a human or humans could be so evil. Eventually after visiting this place along with Natalie and her family we went back to their home in Glavitza. On another occasion we all had such fun it was great. Magda and I also visited Warsaw which is about three hours from her home town.

20th State!

Eventually on the 17th May 05, I made my eleventh visit out to the United States of America. Th is time also making it my twentieth state visited! On arriving to Seattle the same date I dropped off in at my friends. Th is obviously eight hours back with time diff erence.

While in Seattle I made many new friends from the Epilepsy Foundation of Washington. Eventually I went around walking and talking to Americans. Th e funny thing I have always found as mentioned though is Americans always think I am from Australia, New Zealand or Ireland before they fi nally realise the accent is from the United Kingdom. Th e next thing people in the USA always say to me "Do you know the queen?" that really makes me laugh. So "Yeah I took her out for a drink last night." I always say and that totally puzzles them.

Well still on my 05, trip of Washington State I was taken into downtown Seattle. Seeing places like Pike market and Lusty Lady Nude bar. One big thing I fi rst noticed is that Seattle has many Starbuck coff ee shops. Also the streets in Seattle are all so steep. You always need to keep yourself in good shape due to the depth of the roads. Th ere was still plenty to see after this. Th e Space Needle! Th at is something nobody should miss. Climb 520 feet to the observation deck of Seattle's signature building, which is actually 605 feet tall, for spectacular views of the city and its surrounding area. Such as Lake Washington and Queen Ann Hill. It was all good fun with plenty to see. Just like San Francisco!

Towards the end of my fi rst week, I dropped off to see my family in Canada. While there I stayed again in the city of Surrey for two days. Th e fun and excitement of the visit was seeing the soccer again. Th is was on Sunday 22nd May when my relatives took me to see the Vancouver Whitecaps.

While watching the Whitecaps I had the honour of seeing the Lady Whitecaps I had the Excitement of watching them play against Denver ladies! Whitecaps won Vancouver Whitecaps 2-0 Denver Mile High Mustangs. After this game I then had the fun of watching the men play Atlanta Silverbacks. Th ey beat the Silverbacks: Vancouver Whitecaps 4-1 Atlanta Silverbanks.

After the fun in Vancouver I again went back into the state of Washington and into Seattle.

Me by helicopter in Seattle: One other special was my helicopter tour on Wednesday 25th May 05. I did this tour all around the city of Seattle and the mountains around the area.

Seattle helicopter on Wednesday 25th May 05.

Including this you could see so many millions of evergreen trees everywhere. It was an amazing tour visiting lovely mountainous and amazing city in Washington. Th is now my twentieth state of the country I love and always dreamed of visiting since a young child.

Some advice

Do I have to take medicine every day?

Yes. You must take your medicine every day, even when you aren't having seizures or when you think you won't have a seizure. To prevent seizures, you have to take the medicine regularly, just as your doctor tells you.

What should I do if I forget to take my medicine?

The Magic Bullett!!

127

Usually you should take your medicine as soon as you realize you forgot a dose. If more than 24 hours have passed since your last dose, call your doctor for instructions.

Should I take extra medicine if I think I'm about to have a seizure?

No. Th e amount of medicine you take for your epilepsy is carefully set for your own specifi c needs. No extra medicine should be taken without your doctor's approval.

Can I take other drugs while taking medicine for epilepsy?

Because many drugs aff ect the ability of your epilepsy medicine to control your seizures, ask your doctor or pharmacist before taking other drugs, even drugs you can buy without a prescription.

Drinkers who experience blackouts typically drink too much and too quickly, which causes their blood alcohol levels to rise very rapidly.

Fire Alarms!!!

Now then what a way to start and fi nish this chapter of the book. Because on Saturday 16th August 2008, Natalie and me got married. Well the night before the wedding I had to stay at the house of to my mum and dad while Natalie, Kate, Howard, Nicola and Sarah stayed at our house on Pitt Street. Well what a start to the wedding day, I got up and after starting to get ready my Aunty Di made a phone call to me. "Lee can you make Granddad some toast please." She said. So I got the bread out and started doing the toast. I put the bread into the toaster and of course left the room. I went back into the kitchen to see the toast burning. Th en Dottie, who was Howard's mum came in through the door and "Lee, what is that smell what's that burning!" Well I came out of the kitchen stinking of burning smoke. "It is alright Dottie I have just burnt the toast in the kitchen." I said. It had just been the same as before I met Natalie. Where I would constantly be burning and setting things on fi re under the grill in my old flat.

But that was only the start of the day. As I was soon to fi nd out wearing an old designed suite for the wedding, I still don't know how but you could not smell burnt smoke on me. Well there were many of my friends and family at the wedding. After the ceremony all of our family went over to the parks in Staff ord where we had photographs taken.

Natalie & me on wedding day in parks. Magda, Mum & Me on wedding day

Eventually Magda and I along with our family then went onto the reception to do talks and have some fun with our families from England and Poland in Staff ord of the West Midlands. Well, on arriving into Tillington Hall there was a cake and plenty of food for us all to eat. My mate Dave was best man for the wedding. We all had such a good laugh. I knew what the celebration song was to be. So when Dave did his talk, I then mentioned a few things along with Magda's sister and dad. "I was looking back into my diaries and thought to myself. I had two dreams in life.

One was to see West Bromwich Albion at Wembley and the other was to visit America. "I have achieved both of these. "Now I have my own house. "What is next in life?" Th en after the talks and the start of the party a song started and who was it? Well of course Ricky Martin and straight away. So I was straight up "Livin' La Vida Loca!" I jumped and started singing and dancing to it just as I would have been doing at the Grapes in Staff ord or Dallas of America. Th en after the music everybody got together and started talking for the afternoon. More was still to come though on the night while Magda and I stayed at the Tillington Hall hotel.

Because while all were asleep in the hotel fi re alarms went off! Up Natalie and I shot out of bed. Th en both of us tried to get dressed to get out of the room. Well Magda did quite well but me again that is another story. I got out of the bed and tried to put on my clothes. But not forgetting I had been wearing a very ancient form of suite. Well it was not easy to put on these clothes back on to wear. Th is fast to run out of the building, eventually I managed to put my shirt and trousers on. But by then realising it was impossible to put the shoes and all back on fast. Th en Magda and me both ran down the stairs and outside with all of the other people in the hotel outside onto the gardens. Just my luck as outside the hotel it was typical English weather. Th e rain was shooting down from the sky. It was unreal and I then got very wet and cold wearing no shoes. Eventually the alarms went off and everybody was allowed back. Th is back into the hotel and their into the rooms. Th e next day I found out why the alarms went off. Well it was all due to a water leakage in one of the tubes in the kitchen. After that Natalie and I went down to Birmingham for a few days and nights out to celebrate the start of a new life together.

Mr. Innocent.

Well three months later something great and unexpectedly happened just after returning back home from work. Because as I walked into our house in Staff ord on Tuesday 11ᵗʰ November 08. I opened the lounge door and what a big surprise!! Th ere was a little person sitting down alongside with Natalie in the room. Th is small and I mean small boy was a Cuhawaii. I could not believe it. "Who is this?" I said. Well "It is a little dog lee, what do you think about having him? Magda said. I suddenly had this big smile on my face "Yes that would be great, you know I love dogs Natalie." I stated. Th is is little Frank and me in 09 So Magda along with me had a little think. "What shall we call him Lee?" Natalie said. I don't mind, you choose whatever name you want for him. So we had a think and "Frank!" Magda said. So we decided to call the Cuhawaii Frank. He was and still is so small, when we fi rst had him. I would regularly trip over him or sit on him by accident. Th is is due to Frank, and in general Chuawaii's being so small.

He is great constantly of no trouble to anybody unless food appears. Th at's when it is time to say "Oh no here's little Mr Innocent!!

Perseverance

Now then I have never dwelled on reversals: a defeated bill or a legislative cause that remains unrealised year after year; a medical condition that has tried to defeat me but never will. Th ere has been so much to be thankful for. Th ere have been so many reasons to hope.

I have many long time friends among the world: United States of America, Canada, Poland, other parts of Europe and the Great Britain. And I have come to respect the National Health Services around the world. All of these whether doctors, neurologists or surgeons. I never held back from my fi nal operation. As I have said many times, I was waiting to see who was capable of lifting up and inspiring our nation to move forward, toward our highest and best ideals, before I decide to give my opinion of anyone. On the morning of my operation I new that I would have the capacity to inspire. I was and still am among the millions of people that have moved forward having gone through a disability of some form. I have been moved about the many that have gone and achieved so much while suff ering around my uplifting appeal. But I have come to believe that all concerning the medical profession around the world will be needed now at this time and in our future to come. After returning from Kings College Hospital on Wednesday 17th January 07. As I talked with Mr Richard Selway and Professor Polkey, I saw the impact that all of the words were having on us. Th is after fi nding out that Mr Richard Selway could burn a hole around the brain tumour. Also explaining that I was to be the first person to undergo this form of operation. After telling me this it made me ask what would be the success from the operation. "Well, we can erase the tumour totally to cure you of your epilepsy, but your memory would totally go. "Or we can reduce the tumour which would cure you of your giggling aura stomach sensations and reduce the severity of the epileptic seizures. Well I felt more certain that the future would hand me a new beginning. Even though being the fi fteenth person to undergo this form of brain surgery.

So I had a think and "If the operation can take away these frustrating giggling stomach sensations. Th en I will undergo the operation to reduce the seizures. As I do not want to loose my memory that would cause problems which are not worth having. I can cope with light forms of epileptic seizures but not being cured and ending up unable to know what is going on and how to emotionally cope with anything.

Th is due the tumour being on my left temporal lobe. Th is of which controls my memory and emotions.

My family and I have fought on with extraordinary determination and skill, and have never kept the outcome around health problems come into the future. By that time, of course, I was recovering from my successful surgery at Kings College Hospital in London, and soon get well enough to move into Magda and my new property. Th at hope came true, as did going back into work, doing my arobics and watching the soccer in West Bromwich. Th e work I went into was more care work. Later in the year Families and so many friends of mine came over to see an unbelievably happy family to celebrate Christmas and the happy new year with Natalie, my family and me in Staff ord for Christmas from Glavitza in Poland.

And speaking of hope, I still recall that fi rst evening after my seizure at Staff ord College: eating fi sh and chips from the local chip shop with

Mum and Howard and watching my soccer team West Bromwich Albion. Th en later the American comedy shows Mauri and Jerry Springer on television. But not even someone as hopeful as I would have imagined that on 21ˢᵗ of July 1994 I would be standing in the middle of America. Eventually to visit twenty states in the United States of America.

As my story comes to a close, I am still living with epilepsy and on the odd occasion can have a memory relapse.

But I don't dwell on that. I have good days now that Mr Selway has erased the giggling sensations from my stomach. But I also may have days where I could have the odd seizure in my sleep or while awake. Luckily now I am physically able to control the jurking and do not collapse. But more than that day of being diagnosed with it, I have not spent a day in bed. With Natalie and little Frank's constant help and encouragement, I follow a healthy diet and continue to do moderate exercise. I look forward to going out every day, rain or shine, to breathe fresh air. I tire more easily than before and need extra rest, and I sometimes use one word when I mean to use another. Still I continue to watch European soccer or American baseball and football. All of my life, the teachings of respect have provided an understanding to the public of disabilities.

My hopes, and my love of many sports and different countries has always been my inspiration. Those foundations have been shaken at times by tragedy and misfortune, but faith remains fixed in my heart, as it has since my childhood days. It is the most positive force in my life, and the external optimism. I have fallen short in my life, but my determination brought me home.

For almost twenty five years, I have represented people who are facing injustice pain. Life can be violent and grim, but I think of the Resurrection and I feel a sense of hope. When I've started down a spiral of depression or negativism or loss, I've been lucky enough to see another side that can catch me on the same way. I believe that if you have a warm and embracing heart, confidence and determination can have a powerful impact on your outlook. Natalie and Mum have been a great source of strength and love because we share this underlying belief and faith.

Life is eternal. Work continues. It is a calling, an opportunity to do things about injustice or unfairness. It helps to have a goal. I've always tried to have one.

Even having a neurological condition named epilepsy has proved itself an impetus for hope. In my lifetime I have witnessed advances in medical understanding of malignancy and treatment for it that would have been unthinkable in my childhood years. Yet so much more is possible. I see how far we have come around the world in my lifetime. When I was fi rst treated at the Children's hospital in Birmingham of the West Midlands of the United Kingdom in 1975 the National Health Service had hardly been heard of the United Kingdom. Now it is known all around the world. Even in these challenging times, there are daily reasons to be grateful. After years of work, we are now passing a National Health Service bill that will triple in size and dramatically expand opportunities for service to the entire world.

And of course, my work to improve health care, the great work of my life, this will continue to my last day (and beyond if, as I hope, these words inspire readers to take up the cause). One of the great lessons I've learned from a life concerning medical problems is that no reform is ever truly complete. We must constantly keep moving forward, seeking ways to create that more perfect union. In my personal life, I have kept moving forward to avoid the tragedy behind me. As a constant worker, that motivation has been a blessing.

These days, simple pleasures fill me with happiness In my thirty-nine years of life I have never grown tired of sitting and helping people.

Now at this moment in time as I write the book I am sitting at home in Staff ord. I know that at some time in the next few weeks. I will suddenly have quite a hard week. This will be where suddenly out of the blue I have a large amount of epileptic seizures. But since my first operation in 12 they have changed so much. Because I will still have epileptic seizures in my sleep. But the Tonic-Clonic seizures have been reduced and controlled so much in severity.

If my muscles start to stiffen I do not suddenly fall becoming unconscious. What I can now do is just get up out of this chair in the house and walk outside into fresh air.

Then breath in and out slowly this will then slow the muscle spasms and eye twitching down of the seizure. And suddenly out of the blue everything connected to the epileptic seizure stops. I then just walk back into the house make a cup of tea and put the television back on. At another time I may go watching to see the Albion in West Bromwich. Plus of cause laughing and joking with my wife Natalie and little Cuhawaii Frank.

All at the same time as I am enjoyably able to psychologically picture so many happy memories of vacations around the world. These such as the twenty states I have dreamed of visiting and now achieved by going out to America plus Vancouver in Canada. This now dramatically as on Wednesday 27th April 11, I reach a new years of age all without suffering with those giggly tingling sensations I had suffered with since my childhood.

Thanks for reading and I hope you have enjoyed my story around everything time and daily ideas arrive now having my little daughter Natalie looking identical makes my life.

Today now living in property to which has personally paid for it has become fantastic with my little daughter Natalie coming into the world e fantastic,

Lee.

ABOUT THE AUTHOR

I was born in Birmingham of the West Midlands in the United Kingdom on 27th April 1971. Around my thirty-nine years I have seen two sides of life. One side being amazing but the other side has been a nightmare. By reading this you will see everything in my words and also read about medical and world subjects of and around the world.

Printed and bound by PG in the USA

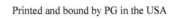

USA2019PGIL